THE GLOBAL STATUS OF THE PROJECT MANAGEMENT PROFESSION

THE GLOBAL STATUS OF THE PROJECT MANAGEMENT PROFESSION

A Report from the
First Global Project Management Forum
New Orleans, Louisiana, USA
October 15, 1995

SPONSORS
BELLSOUTH
CARTER & BURGESS, INC.
INTEGRATED PROJECT SYSTEMS
NCR
STRATEGIC PROJECT DEVELOPMENT, INC.
UNIVERSITY OF SAN DIEGO

Project Management Institute
130 South State Road
Upper Darby, PA 19082 USA
610-734-3330 Fax: 610-734-3266
Internet: pmieo@ix.netcom.com
Web: http://www.pmi.org

The Global Status of the Project Management Profession

Library of Congress Cataloging-in-Publication Data

The global status of the project management profession / [editor-in-chief, James S. Pennypacker ... et al.].
       p.   cm.
    The Global Project Management Forum was held on 10-15-95 at World Trade Center in New Orleans.
    Sponsors AT&T ... [et al.].
    ISBN: 1-880410-34-6
    1. Industrial project management--Congresses.   I. Pennypacker, James S.   II. American Telephone and Telegraph Company.
III. Project Management Institute.   IV. Global Project Management Forum (1995 : World Trade Center of New Orleans)
HD69.P75G564 1996
658.4'04--dc20   96-22526
                                                                                                                    CIP

Copyright ©1996 by the Project Management Institute. All rights reserved. Printed in the United States of America. No part of this work may be reproduced or transmitted in any form or by any means, electronic, manual, photocopying, recording, or by any information storage and retrieval system, without prior written permission of the publisher.

Book Team
Editor-in-Chief
James S. Pennypacker

Graphic Designer	*Editor, Book Division*
Michelle Triggs Owen	Jeannette M. Cabanis
Cover design by	*Associate Editor*
Dewey L. Messer	Sandy Jenkins
Production Coordinator	*Publications Coordinator*
Mark S. Parker	Bobby R. Hensley

PMI books are available at special quantity discounts to use as premiums and sales promotions, or for use in corporate training programs. For more information, please write to the Business Manager, PMI Communications, 40 Colonial Square, Sylva, NC 28779. Or contact your local bookstore.

The paper used in this book complies with the Permanent Paper Standard issued by the National Information Standards Organization (Z39.48—1984).

10 9 8 7 6 5 4 3 2 1

The Global Status of the Project Management Profession

CONTENTS

PREFACE   VII

INTRODUCTION   IX

PART I: A WINDOW ON THE WORLD: REPORTS FROM PARTICIPATING COUNTRIES   1

Australia/Western Australia   3, 9
Brazil   12
Canada   15
Colombia   19
Czech Republic   23
Egypt   27
France   29
Germany   33
Greece   36
India   39
Indonesia   43
Ireland   47
Israel   51
Italy   53
Japan   59
Korea   63
Kuwait   66
Mexico   69
New Zealand   72
Norway   77
Pakistan   80
Russia   84
Saudi Arabia   90
South Africa   95
Spain   98
Turkey   100
United Kingdom   103
United States   106
Venezuela   110

PART II: PRESENTATIONS BY DISTINGUISHED SPEAKERS 115

Introduction 117
Peter Morris: *Project Management: An International Profession* 118
Kent Crawford: *Global Issues: The Project Management Institute's View* 124
Klaus Pannenbäcker: *Globalization of Project Management* 126
Alan Stretton: *The Global Project Management Body of Knowledge and Standards* 130
Hiroshi Tanaka: *Project Management Standards in Japan and ENAA Cooperation with Asian Countries* 131
Brian Kooyman: *Global Project Management Certification* 135
Paul Dinsmore: *Project Management in Latin America* 139
Vladimir I. Voropajev: *Project Management in Emerging Economies* 141
Robert Youker: *Project Management Support of Economic Development* 149

PART III: THE GROUP PROCESS—REPORTS FROM THE BREAKOUT SESSIONS 151

Introduction 153
Global Project Management Body of Knowledge 154
International Project Management Standards 155
Global Project Management Certifications 156
Communications Among Project Management Professionals and Organizations 157
Global Project Management Cooperation and Organization 159

PART IV: CONCLUSIONS AND NEXT STEPS 161

Contacts 162
Global Forum Survey Results 164
How to Participate 167
IMPA '96 Global PM Forum—Paris 168
PMI '96 Global PM Forum—Boston 169

PART V: SPONSORS OF THE 1995 GLOBAL FORUM 171

BellSouth 173
Carter & Burgess, Inc. 174
Integrated Project Systems 175
NCR 176
Strategic Project Development, Inc. 177
University of San Diego 178

PART VI: ATTENDEES OF THE 1995 GLOBAL FORUM 179

List of Attendees 181

PREFACE

Brian Fletcher

THE SHORT HISTORY of the people and associations in the project management movement includes many notable events. Their significance often results from being a "first": an inaugural meeting, a new attendance record, an innovative standards publication, a proclamation, emergence of new technology, a milestone occurrence, etc.

The October 1995 Global Project Management Forum, convened at the top of the World Trade Center in New Orleans, was a memorable happening for similar reasons and more. It was a major milestone and time will increase its importance and recognition as a watershed event in the history of the project management profession.

For the first time, many world leaders in the fraternity assembled in one place. Although the gathering took place in the United States, over half of those in attendance represented a country outside the USA. All brought a message. Many came to address their colleagues but above all else, they came to participate in the exchange. It is an understatement to say that the very best of today's project management pacesetters from every corner of the globe came to hear, speak and contribute.

Like the people who came from around the world, the project management organizations with whom they were associated were equally spread across the globe; from New Zealand to Canada, from Moscow to Japan. Some societies were newly emerging and on their way to becoming prominent elements within an ever-expanding global profession. Many of us with singular language skills recognized our good fortune and were grateful to our colleagues with multi-language skills, that communications throughout were in English.

The Forum was born out of grassroots movements. While almost all participants were aligned with some form of project management society, the emphasis was on contribution. The organizations and the people, meeting as equals, acknowledged themselves to be members of a world-wide family of project management experts, professionals and organizations. It was truly global.

Two questions were posed to the assembly. The evaluation of the results affirmed the mutual desire to be professionals, to build a profession of project management, to promote professionalism in project management through further forums, with minimal administration and maximum learning-by-sharing. Within the practical and cultural limits, these goals were pronounced: working towards global standards and world-wide accepted certification.

This book includes all the Country Reports, together with transcripts of the formal speeches, augmented with break-out session reports. Within the writings will be found all that is unique to culture and country but also much in evidence will be those things that we share in common. All are notable because within the messages and texts will be the benchmarks against which future achievements will be evaluated. The readings will certainly help those who attended to reflect again on what transpired. In addition, the readings will provide those who missed the opportunity to be in New Orleans to catch some of the flavor. In either case, this book will provide an understanding of what took place and serve to improve appreciation for the enthusiasm and spirit of the first Global Project Management Forum.

It is a excellent record of an outstanding, historic event.

Brian Fletcher, P.Eng, is the director of ABRINN Project Management. He is a member of AACE, the Association of Iron and Steel Engineers, the Institute of Mechanical Engineers (UK), and a Fellow of the Project Management Institute, as well as a past president and chairman of PMI. During more than forty years in heavy industry and over twenty-five years in project management training and consulting, he has worked on assignments in Russia, South Africa, Canada, the U.S. and throughout Europe.

The Global Status of the Project Management Profession

INTRODUCTION

David L. Pells

I CONSIDER IT A great honor and my privilege to introduce the PMI '95 Global Project Management Forum and this Global Report, a first-ever attempt at obtaining a status of the project management profession around the world. Perhaps it has been a presumptuous attempt. It is true that not all countries or even regions of the world are reflected in this document, or were represented at the first Global Forum in New Orleans. The Country Reports submitted by professional project management associations and experts from around the world and collected in this volume, however, provide a truly international and honest perspective on the status of our profession in those regions of the earth represented.

Project management experts and practitioners from various countries have been meeting and cooperating professionally for many years. For the past five years at each annual meeting of the Project management Institute (PMI) in North America or the International Project Management Association (IPMA) in Europe, groups of project management friends and colleagues from different countries and continents have been discussing global communication and cooperation with greater and greater intensity. For me personally, those meetings and discussions about global cooperation reached a near-climax at PMI '94 in Vancouver, Canada. In Vancouver two significant sets of meetings occurred. One was a formal meeting of representatives of PMI, IPMA, The Association of Project Managers (APM) from the United Kingdom, and The Australian Institute of Project Management (AIPM) based in Sydney. These organizations discussed formal cooperation on several global issues, including standards, certification, and formation of a global project management organization or "confederation."

> New Orleans is proud to affiliate with the project management profession ... We are a global business city, with one of the largest and most technologically advanced ports in the world. In addition to our maritime industries we have an elaborate infrastructure of railroads, highways, airports, oil and gas facilities, [and] healthcare facilities ... Enjoy our city and come back to do business in New Orleans.
>
> Sandra Ross, Office of the Mayor of New Orleans

Another group of individuals, from approximately a dozen countries, met on a less formal and more personal basis, intensely discussing more cooperation and communication among project management professionals around the world. This second group, of which I was a participant, even established a formal declaration of intent and support.

After PMI '94, on reflecting upon these global issues and the discussions with my project management colleagues around the world, I realized three things. First, global cooperation and communication should be between and among both project management organizations and individual professionals. Second, that communication and cooperation should be open and with as many participant viewpoints and cultures represented as possible. Third, I felt the general PMI membership and attendees at PMI '94 were missing out on an exciting and rewarding opportunity to learn and grow. That is, those not in our meetings didn't know what they were missing. Upon discussing these issues with Brian Fletcher in Canada, Bruce Rodrigues in South Africa, Paul Dinsmore in Brazil, and many others around North America, it seemed appropriate to propose a more formal setting and opportunity for these discussions. The PMI '95 Global Project Management Forum was the result.

From the beginning The Global Forum was intended to achieve several objectives. It was clearly an opportunity for the world's leading project management associations to take another major step towards achieving agreements on international standards, recognition of project management certifications, and development of a global core Project Management Body of Knowledge (PMBOK). It was also intended to bring more project management organizations and experts into this globalization process. Just as importantly, however, the PMI '95 Global Forum offered individual project management experts and interested professionals an opportunity to listen, learn, and actively particulate in the serious and tremendously important discussions.

The first Global Project Management Forum, held at PMI '95 in New Orleans, achieved all of these objectives and more. Over 30 countries were represented, with representatives of national and international project management associations presenting status reports and perspectives on the status of the project management profession in their respective regions. Nearly 200 project management experts and attendees came together for the first time to listen and share with their colleagues from around the world.

Speakers included both the expected and the unexpected, with many countries represented in such a forum for the first time. For me personally, this was the most rewarding aspect, as we heard and saw the pride and excitement in the presentations by representatives of such countries as Brazil, Colombia, the Czech Republic, Indonesia, Malaysia and Mexico. Many in the audience heard for the first time from such truly global project management experts as Peter Morris of the U.K., Klaus Pannenbäcker of Germany, Alan Stretton of Australia, Adesh Jain of India, Hiroshi Tanaka of Japan and Vladimir Voropajev of Russia.

Finally, all Global Forum participants—speakers and audience alike—had the opportunity to join afternoon breakout sessions to discuss five important topics: international project management standards, globally-recognized project management certification, global communication among project management professional organizations, global cooperation and organization of the project management profession, and development of a global core project management body of knowledge. Each of the final discussion groups was attended by 30–40 people.

The success of the first global project management forum was reflected in the congratulations, smiles and applause at the closing plenary session on that Sunday in New Orleans. We all made new friends and learned a great deal in the process. The discussion groups are continuing as global working groups on the same five subject areas. A Global Forum has been established on the Worldwide Web (WWW), using both PMI's webpage and IPMA's (Nordnet) addressees. Most importantly the attendees in New Orleans noted the mandate—do it again. Global Forums will now be held in 1996 at the IMPA '96 World Congress on Project Management in Paris, France (June 24-26), and at the PMI '96 Annual Seminar/Symposium in Boston, Mass., USA (October 4–10).

This book is a summary and culmination of the PMI '95 Global Project Management Forum. It is intended to document the results, but to also be a significant product unto itself. For those of you unable to experience the PMI '95 Global Forum in person, the speakers and country reports contained herein will be both conversational and entertaining. For those of you interested in actually participating in the globalization of the project management profession, you will find contact names, numbers and information.

And for those readers who represent organizations in need of better project management assistance or training, in whatever business or government, I especially encourage you to use this book. It is the first serious attempt to gain a status of the project management profession around the world, and from the first country report received it was clear that new, refreshing and important information was being shared. Needs are different in different countries. The status of the project management profession varies widely. Cultural differences are real. For instance, in some languages there is not yet a word for "management," so how do we teach project management?

This decade has truly seen amazing changes around the world. Just as project management is often described as change management, so must our profession also adapt to our changing environment. We live in a global economy. We are learning to address global social and economic problems through international cooperation. Even on international projects, partnering, teamwork, and cultural integration have become common. Today we can see how project management can become on of the first truly global professions of the twenty-first century. we have the opportunity, and perhaps even the obligation, to make that happen, as leaders and experts in a set of skills the world needs badly. I hope the PMI '95 Global Forum will be the first of many. I hope the Country Reports and information contained in this volume are as interesting and useful to you as they are to me.

> To combine the international languages of humor and project management, I'd like everyone to stand up, shake hands with your neighbor and, in your native language, say "You want it when??"
>
> Roger Glaser, PMI

Finally, while I received many thanks and congratulations after the Global Forum in New Orleans, I want to extend my own appreciation to my fellow PMI Board members, without whose support this project could not have proceeded. I want to also thank Brian Fletcher in Ontario and Bruce Rodrigues in Johannesburg whose constant faxes and support helped maintain the momentum. I especially want to thank Saralee Newell, PMI '95 Seminar/Symposium Project Manager, for her continuous support and for finding the Plimsoll Club at the New Orleans World Trade Center for this important international event. And a special thanks to Sandra Ross from Mayor Mark Morial's office for getting the city solidly behind PMI and for making the Global Forum official, extending the key to the city to our international guests.

Most of all I want to extend a heartfelt "thank you" to those international participants and representatives of project management associations around the world who proved their commitment to a global project management profession by crossing oceans and continents to be in New Orleans in October, 1995. Let us maintain the vision and energy and meet again in 1996. Let the rest of the world join us!

David L. Pells, Vice President-Public Relations, PMI
Project Manager — PMI '95 Global Forum
Member, APM (United Kingdom)
Member, SOVNET (Russia)

PART I

A WINDOW ON THE WORLD

REPORTS FROM PARTICIPATING COUNTRIES

The Global Status of the Project Management Profession

The Global Status of the Project Management Profession

AUSTRALIA

STATUS OF THE PROJECT MANAGEMENT PROFESSION

In general, at what stage is the project management profession in your country today (i.e., newly introduced, growing, mature)? Please comment.

Project management in Australia can be considered somewhere between the level of growing and mature. Maturity has been reached in the development and application of project management techniques and tools in industries such as defense, construction, and information technology. The level is "growing" in the wider range of industries (such as telecommunications and process manufacturing). An assessment by industry would be as follows:

- Engineering and civil construction: Mature, with 25–30 years practice.
- Building construction: Mature, with 20–25 years practice.
- Information technology: Growing, but embracing project management techniques over the last 10 years.
- Telecommunications: Newly introduced, but catching up rapidly, particularly through the AIPM competency development.
- Manufacturing: At best, "newly introduced."
- Defense procurement: Totally embracing project management principles, probably assessed as still growing.
- Research and development: Possible loss of government support means R & D is turning to project management techniques to support commercial-type operations—newly introduced.
- Public service: At all levels have actively been embracing project management techniques for 20 years. Reaching maturity.

> G'day! Australia has a small population of about 18 million in an area the size of the U.S. mainland. Therefore, we must concentrate on productivity. Thus, our government has insisted that any certification for our project managers must be competency-based.
>
> Brian Kooyman, AIPM

What industries or types of projects are the main users of modern project management in your country or region today?

- Engineering and civil construction
- Building construction
- Information technology
- Oil and petroleum
- Defense procurement
- Public service.

Project management techniques are primarily aimed at capital works procurement. However, there is an increasing awareness amongst corporations of using the concept of internal management by projects. The driving force for this is to create leaner organizations to cope with limited resources and keep overheads at a minimum.

What industries or areas of application in your country have the greatest need for more or better project management? What industries or organizations offer the greatest opportunities for growth of professional project management in your country? Why?

The privatization/competition of telecommunications will encourage the implementation of project management techniques in this industry. Similarly research and development organizations will seek to use project management techniques. The manufacturing industry struggles to compete in a region that is rapidly becoming industrialized (i.e., Southeast Asia.) There is still some time required before this industry will move positively towards project management. Organizations will become more project-oriented in the way they do business.

How can the project management profession be most effectively advanced in your country?

Through the initiatives of AIPM and the Western Australian Project Management Association (WAPMA) in association with Australian industry and government. The AIPM, in conjunction with industry (over 55 different industry organizations) and supported by the Australian government, has now completed the "final draft" of the Australian Project Management Competency Standards. This document is the basis for a consistent method of assessment for all those who wish to be involved in the project management environment. These generic standards will be taken by specific industries to develop the industry-specific standards for their project management and workplace reform. This concept and the philosophy of levels of assessment have already been well explained to PMI this year at both the Philadelphia and Sydney meetings, and I would refer you to PMI representatives for a full explanation.

AIPM will also continue to promote activities such as workshops, seminars, and a twice yearly major conference and the implementation of accreditation in Australia with the "Registered Project Manager" award.

What impact will globally recognized project management standards or certification have on the project management profession in your country?

Globally recognized standards will be welcomed by Australian project management professionals, provided they incorporate the current AIPM membership criteria and are based on the national Competency Standards. No global accreditation system can be recognized in Australia by the government unless it is based on the Project Management Competency Standards. This is the fundamental reason why AIPM was considering bringing our accreditation process and competency standards to the table for global cooperation.

ISSUES OF COMMON GLOBAL INTEREST

What should be contained in a global Project Management Body of Knowledge (PMBOK)?

The revised Project Management Body of Knowledge and the Core Framework for Project Management Knowledge, as currently being finalized by representatives of PMI, IPMA,

AIPM, APM, and ENAA are documents that which we believe should be a basis for a global PMBOK. Our only concern is that this document should reflect what industry sees as the performance criteria for competent project management.

Also contained or related to the PMBOK should be globally acceptable Competency Standards that provide a series of internationally recognized levels of competency to allow "transportable" accreditation for project management professionals.

How important will international "Standards" for project management be in your country or region? Please comment.

Within the general Australian project management context, global standards would have little impact. There is already a basic standard virtually developed for national accreditation, and this is government recognized.

The value of global "Standards" will be transportable accreditation for individual members offshore and for multi-national organizations.

Is project management certification of interest in your country? What type of project management certification?

Yes, project management certification is the primary objective of AIPM. The certification must be competency-based, related to knowledge, skill and attribute. As mentioned previously, AIPM has virtually completed the National Competency Standards, and these will be the basis of assessing project management operations to various levels of competency. It is planned that the award of Registered PM (to recognize Professional Project Managers) will be offered in early 1996.

Regarding PMP certification, there is limited interest in Australia, although AIPM has been keen to incorporate the PMP exam into our process so as to potentially allow some recognition of negotiations and the attitude of PMI.

What is your interest or position on a unified global project management association or organization? If you support such an organization, how should it be organized and for what objectives?

AIPM has always supported unified global project management cooperation. We have indicated this by our financial and human resource support toward the global project management discussions in Vancouver, Philadelphia and Sydney. I must add that it is becoming increasingly difficult to report to the AIPM Board that there is a continuing cost benefit.

AIPM has promoted, from the outset, the need to establish international standards of Knowledge, Competence and Accreditation. The benefits have already been stated and must surely be obvious. However, if this is to occur, then a commonality for accreditation standards must be agreed upon by those organizations undertaking accreditation and those about to embrace accreditation. It is my opinion that this factor is what controls the "window of opportunity" for creating global standards and agreement. If we wait too long, institutes will become entrenched and lose the flexibility to adapt.

Discussions to date indicate that this window is still open, and that there is a commonality that can be exploited.

The role of any agreements or umbrella association must be limited to that of developing and maintaining international standards for knowledge, skill, attribute and, as a result, levels of international recognition for certification.

The fundamental of any global cooperation must remain with national institutes. National, because socio-cultural identities of each country and their individual styles of project management must be recognized and respected. Thus any global association must have a limited function that responds to the needs of national project management institutes. This is already a problem that faces PMI and IPMA—it cannot be ignored!

At this stage we are ambivalent about whether the National Institutes should be arranged in region or industry groupings or whatever. This is part of the mechanics of a process; the best method will become apparent when the concept and objectives are established.

How can project management associations around the world better communicate and cooperate to advance the project management profession?

The answer lays in what the global project management cooperation discussions are all about: to create an association, or agreements that allow the world's project management professionals a forum in which to coordinate activities and communicate. The Internet in itself is not an answer!

Those of us fortunate enough to have been involved in recent discussion between PMI, IPMA, APM and AIPM, where a common theme was being discussed, have learned and gained much.

YOUR ORGANIZATION

Briefly describe the history, purpose, organization and activities of the professional project management organization you represent.

The Australian Institute of Project Management (AIPM) evolved from a group known as the Project Managers Forum, which was established in 1976. The success and growth of the Forum led to the formation of the AIPM in 1989.

The Institute is the only national body that serves as a unifying influence for industries that manage projects.

The Institute is a voluntary body, working for the benefit of its members.

VISION

"… to encourage Professionalism in Project Management …"

OBJECTIVES

The objectives of the AIPM are to:
- Promote a professional approach to project management
- Advance the discipline of project management
- Promote the self-development of Project Managers and members of project teams
- Encourage the study of project management
- Increase public awareness of the value of project management.

AIMS

In its pursuit of professionalism in project management, the Institute aims to provide the following services:
- Dissemination of best practice information on project management
- Continuing education seminars and workshops
- Accreditation of project management education and training courses
- Certification of Project Managers as project management professionals
- Maintenance of national competency standards
- A Code of Ethics for Project Managers.

CHAPTERS AND AFFILIATIONS

Most activities of the Institute are undertaken at chapter level. Chapters are established in Adelaide, Brisbane, Canberra, Melbourne, and Sydney, with a growing demand for chapters in Hobart and Darwin. The Western Australian Project Management Association (WAPMA) works closely with the AIPM.

The Institute has a cooperative agreement with the Project Management Institute (PMI) in North America, and maintains close liaison with the Association of Project Managers (APM) in the UK, and IPMA in Europe.

BENEFITS OF MEMBERSHIP

Seminars and Workshops

Chapters conduct ongoing programs of seminars and workshops on typical issues relevant to project management and to highlight interesting projects, both local and overseas. Workshops are held to update members on specific tools and techniques of project management. Seminars and workshops promote an environment of fellowship and the opportunity for business and social contact with peers and other working project managers.

Publications

Members, Associates and Students automatically receive the *Australian Project Manager,* the official journal of the Australian Institute of Project Management. Overseas Associates may also receive the journal for a small fee to cover postage and handling. Chapters publish a regular newsletter to inform members of local activities and news.

National Conferences

A national conference is held bi-annually and provides the opportunity to benefit from new ideas and techniques and to meet and make contact with others interested and involved in project management.

Personal and Professional Development

As well as broadening and deepening their knowledge of project management by attendance at seminars, workshops and conferences, members can serve on a chapter's standing and special purpose committees to work with others in promoting professionalism in project management.

MEMBERSHIP OF THE INSTITUTE

All people with an interest in project management are encouraged to join the Institute.

The Australian Institute of Project Management has the following Grades of Membership:

- Honorary Fellows who are distinguished persons whom the Institute wishes to honor
- Fellows who have made a significant contribution to the profession of project management
- Members who are or have been practicing project managers with demonstrated qualifications and experience
- Associates who have a substantial interest in project management
- Overseas Associates with an interest in project management may be affiliated with the Institute
- Students who are enrolled in an appropriate course of study.

In addition, the Institute provides for:

- Registered Project Managers who meet professional standards set by the Institute
- Company Associate. Companies and other organizations can become affiliated with the Institute. This affiliation allows financial sponsorship of individuals as Fellows, Members, Associates and Students at reduced subscription fees.

Certain grades of membership entitle members to vote, use post nominals and participate in committees.

Does your organization have established relations with agencies or departments of your government, or with universities? Please describe.

Yes, AIPM has strong relationships with various levels of government departments. We have membership levels with Department of Defense, Australian Construction Services, and Telecom.

We also have responsibility limits/levels through the project management Competency Standards to the "National Training Board" and the "Australian National Training Authority."

AIPM has encouraged and established links with the University of Technology (Sydney), University of N.S.W., Queensland University of Technology, Royal Melbourne Institute of Technology, South Australian University, and others. AIPM has produced a draft "Reference Curriculum" for Master of Project Management courses. These universities are asking AIPM to provide accreditation for their project management courses.

WESTERN AUSTRALIA

STATUS OF THE PROJECT MANAGEMENT PROFESSION

In general, at what stage is the project management profession in your country today (i.e., newly introduced, growing, mature)? Please comment.

The project management profession in our region is at a growing stage in most industries and fairly mature in some industries.

What industries or types of projects are the main users of modern project management in your country or region today?

The following industries are represented by our membership and use modern project management to some extent:

- Building
- Utilities
- Defense
- Construction
- Consulting
- Public works
- Transportation
- Information technology.

Some industries tend to use modern project management, which is often controlled by multinational engineering firms.

What industries or areas of application in your country have the greatest need for more or better project management? What industries or organizations offer the greatest opportunities for growth of professional project management in your country? Why?

The resources sector, in particular the mining industry, and local and state government change programs, have the greatest need for more or better project management.

Many organizations, both private and government, are following a worldwide trend of "managing by projects" and as such have a need to heighten their awareness and skills in project management. However, many (maybe most) of these organizations are not consciously aware that what they are doing could be enhanced with the application of project management principles, techniques and tools.

> Our organization operates in the state of Western Australia (which is not a separate country, although there are those in Perth who might prefer it that way!). We have 81 PMPs and a membership of 230; out of only 1.5 million people, that is a very high per capita representation. One trend we see in our area is an expansion into so-called soft projects, with less tangible deliverables, such as organizational change projects.
>
> Jim Lyon, WAPMA

How can the project management profession be most effectively advanced in your country?

The project management profession here can be best advanced by continuing our Project Management Professional (PMP) program and support for the Masters in Project Management at Curtin University. Continue to work with the AIPM to develop a nationally accepted set of project management competencies based on those areas as outlined in PMI's *Guide to the Project Management Body of Knowledge*.

What impact will globally recognized project management standards or certification have on the project management profession in your country?

Our membership has a stake in the recognition of any global project management standards and/or certification. WAPMA has successfully conducted 3 series of workshops leading to the PMP examination. One hundred and two members have attended these workshops. Ninety-four of these have sat for the PMP exam. The programs run in 1993 and 1994 produced a total of 50 new PMPs. We are waiting on the results of the 45 members who sat for the exam in June 1995.

While the overall profession of project management will be enhanced by globally recognized standards and/or certification, there is a need to recognize cultural and political differences at a national level. Cooperating and collaborating with other project management organizations is the only way to have a single and truly globally recognized professional certification.

ISSUES OF COMMON GLOBAL INTEREST

What should be contained in a global Project Management Body of Knowledge (PMBOK)?

Those knowledge areas of project management that are common across international boundaries.

How important will international "Standards" for project management be in your country or region? Please comment.

See "What impact will globally recognized ..." above.

Is project management certification of interest in your country? What type of project management certification?

See "What impact will globally recognized ..." above. There is a need for certification of project management professionals, with PMI's PMP as a model. There is also a need for a more stringent certification of those persons who perform the duties of the project manager, with AIPM's Registered Project Manager as a model.

What is your interest or position on a unified global project management association or organization? If you support such an organization, how should it be organized and for what objectives?

WAPMA fully supports open communications and cooperation between professional project associations/institutes as well as individual project management professionals.

WAPMA prefers a federation of national associations/institutes. Subject to further study, an organization modeled on the International Council of Management Consulting

Institutes (ICMCI) is preferred. There are currently 20 member associations/institutes in the ICMCI. The ICMCI consists of 6 elected officers, and one or more voting representatives per member association, depending upon the size of their organization. This federation could be called the "International Council of Project Management Institutes" ("ICPMI").

The objectives of a global organization should include the following:
- A uniform body of knowledge
- A recognized world-class certification for project management professionals
- Full reciprocity between national associations/institutes
- Mentoring and nurturing professional associations in developing countries
- Enabling project management professionals to practice freely across national boundaries.

How can project management associations around the world better communicate and cooperate to advance the project management profession?

The "ICPMI's" web site on the Internet would enhance communications between member institutes and individual project management professionals. Cooperation can only be achieved when the member institutes can put aside their purely nationalist views and prejudices.

YOUR ORGANIZATION

Briefly describe the history, purpose, organization and activities of the professional project management organization you represent.

WAPMA was formed in 1982 by individuals from the building and property development industries. Its membership now has a much broader base with members from more state government bodies in transportation and utilities. There is also a smaller, but growing, membership from other industries such as information technology, manufacturing, engineering consulting and project management consulting.

WAPMA is administered by a Council that has an executive function and committees that are active in such areas as practice, education, membership and standards. It also liaises with national and international project bodies. It has the following classes of membership and current members:

Life Members-2; Fellows-0; Members-171; Associate Members-46; Students-1;
TOTAL-220

Does your organization have established relations with agencies or departments of your government, or with universities?

WAPMA was instrumental in the establishment of a Masters in Project Management (MPM) program at Curtin University. The MPM program started in February 1993 and takes 3 years part-time or one and a half years full-time to complete. It has an annual intake of about 20 students each year, with the first graduates in December 1995. WAPMA continues to play a supporting role in this MPM program.

The Global Status of the Project Management Profession

BRAZIL

STATUS OF THE PROJECT MANAGEMENT PROFESSION

In general, at what stage is the project management profession in your country today (i.e., newly introduced, growing, mature)? Please comment.

Project management was first used in Brazil during the 1960s by Petrobras, a Brazilian oil company that learned it from their foreign contractors. The idea of project management as a profession started during the 1970s with the development of petrochemical industries. During that time we had a PMI Brazilian Chapter with more than 250 members for more than six years. Project management concepts are well known in general areas.

> A headline on a recent Brazilian newspaper read '4,000 Projects Unfinished.' In order to change this trend, we are going to privatize our economy, and we will need a lot of project managers.
>
> Marcio Prieto, PMI

What industries or types of projects are the main users of modern project management in your country or region today?

Petrochemicals, oil, construction, hydroelectric, banks, contractors and designers are the most advanced in the area of project management practices. Nowadays, the Government Sector, which controls telecommunication, mail, air traffic, airports, railroads, roads, hospitals, universities and others, leads in developing the growth of project management methodologies.

What industries or areas of application in your country have the greatest need for more or better project management? What industries or organizations offer the greatest opportunities for growth of professional project management in your country? Why?

The greatest opportunities come from the Government Sector, which needs to achieve their political and public services objectives with more efficiency. But all sectors of the Brazilian economy could benefit from modern project management concepts.

How can the project management profession be most effectively advanced in your country?

First, by establishing professional management standards in order to have a basis for professional certification. Second, by obtaining government acknowledgment of the certification process. Third, through exchange of ideas and knowledge among project management professionals. Fourth, by developing training, seminars, university programs, and so on.

What impact will globally recognized project management standards or certification have on the project management profession in your country?

The formal recognition of project management as a profession of the future, because the standards would be meaningful and truly professional.

ISSUES OF COMMON GLOBAL INTEREST

What should be contained in a global Project Management Body of Knowledge (PMBOK)?

The essential thing that could be common to the international community related to project management would be a Global Project Management Body of Knowledge as a general guideline.

This Global PMBOK should be open so that individual national organizations could include their particular standards, practices and reference documents to be used in setting up a national PMP certification program. This way, we could maintain the diverse cultural and language characteristics of early organization with a common universal classification system.

How important will international "Standards" for project management be in your country or region? Please comment?

It is very important that they be recognized as a profession, but must be accountable to the Brazilian Government, which rules all the professions in the country.

Is project management certification of interest in your country? What type of project management certification?

There is great interest in project management certification, which could start immediately, along with the necessary steps to obtain the government approval.

What is your interest or position on a unified global project management association or organization? If you support such an organization, how should it be organized and for what objectives?

A unified global project management organization should:
- be a federation of national entities
- provide acceptance of project management around the world
- be in service to member country organizations
- work to establish a universal project management classification system
- provide PMP certifications tailored by national organizations
- set international project management standards
- be non-aligned with any country
- not be dominated by any one national organization.

> In 1982, the Brazil chapter of PMI was one of the Outstanding Chapters at the PMI Seminar/Symposium. By 1984, it was defunct ... [now] we need contacts between universities in the States and universities in Brazil; we need companies to specify project management requirements in contracts carried out in Brazil in order to impress on the Brazilian government that project management is important.
>
> Jose Augusto Neves,
> Dinsmore & Associates

How can project management associations around the world better communicate and cooperate to advance the project management profession?

At the moment in our country via fax communications, but soon via the Internet.

YOUR ORGANIZATION

Briefly describe the history, purpose, organization and activities of the professional project management organization you represent.

There is not a project management organization in Brazil. We are members and representatives in several associations that apply project management practices to achieve their objectives and foster the exchange of ideas and knowledge among project management practitioners.

Does your organization have established relations with agencies or departments of your government, or with universities?

We are part of the development of project management in Brazil (the only books related to project management published in Portuguese were written by a member of our organization, Paul Dinsmore). We are very close to the development of project management and practice on the Government Sector and working together with universities, agencies, and professional organizations.

CANADA

STATUS OF THE PROJECT MANAGEMENT PROFESSION

In general, at what stage is the project management profession in your country today (i.e., newly introduced, growing, mature)? Please comment.

Project management in Canada can be traced back to the 1920s, primarily in connection with infrastructure and industrial projects. Since then, the large share of Canada's Gross Domestic Product that has been allocated to these capital-intensive areas has contributed to the development of the project management profession.

Today, project management practices can be found in virtually all business and government sectors. Despite a growing knowledge base, there remain many opportunities where project management practices can be applied (e.g., in "soft" or "management" projects).

What industries or types of projects are the main users of modern project management in your country or region today?

Capital projects within the industrial sector are the most advanced in the use of project management practices. Owners, designers, contractors, and manufacturers have, over the years, developed effective project management methodologies that which have evolved into a common set of business practices.

With the increased recognition and promotion of project management as a profession, modern project management concepts are quickly expanding into other sectors. While not as prevalent as in other areas, the government sector has seen a growth in project management in the procurement and construction areas.

> Our objective is to grow project management in Canada. We are now graduating 60 graduate students per year in project management. But to obtain public recognition, we will need government recognition, which in Canada must be done province by province.
>
> David Smith, PMI-Canada

What industries or areas of application in your country have the greatest need for more or better project management? What industries or organizations offer the greatest opportunities for growth of professional project management in your country? Why?

All sectors could benefit from improved project management. Opportunities for growth should come with industry's awareness of project management and the advantages of applying project management practices to achieve their business objectives.

How can the project management profession be most effectively advanced in your country?

The project management profession can most effectively advance by establishing professional project management standards as the basis for professional certification and by having provincial governments—as the "professional" authority in Canada—acknowledge the certification process as a meaningful professional standard.

University programs, research in project management, training, and fostering the exchange of ideas and knowledge amongst project management practitioners are other avenues for developing the profession.

What impact will globally recognized project management standards or certification have on the project management profession in your country?

Provided that the standards are meaningful and at a truly professional level, the impact would be a very positive one. If, however, the standards are trivial in the eyes of the international project management community, then there could be a very negative impact.

ISSUES OF COMMON GLOBAL INTEREST

What should be contained in a global Project Management Body of Knowledge (PMBOK)?

Given the diverse cultural and language characteristics of the international project management community, it would be difficult to define a "global Project Management Body of Knowledge." However, it is possible to establish a common, universal classification system that could be used to categorize the emerging body of knowledge. With a global classification system, the effort to organize, retrieve and use the body of knowledge is greatly reduced.

In addition, consideration should be given to providing general guidelines for the use of individual national organizations, outlining the particular standards, practices, and reference documents to be used in setting up a national PMP certification program.

How important will international "Standards" for project management be in your country or region? Please comment.

Project management standards are essential if the intent is to be recognized as a "profession." However, if standards are established, then project management professionals must be prepared to be held accountable (e.g., in a court of law) for meeting those standards—a very important area and one that cannot be treated lightly.

Is project management certification of interest in your country? What type of project management certification?

The phenomenal interest in PMI's certification program is a good indicator of the general interest in project management certification. If a meaningful certification standard can be established—with government recognition—then there is certain to be a widespread and strong interest in obtaining the credential.

What is your interest or position on a unified global project management association or organization? If you support such an organization, how should it be organized and for what objectives?

A global project management association represents a unique opportunity at this point in time. Provided that it is properly structured, such an association can bring together an emerging profession on a consistent basis around the world. One can imagine having a national professional designation that is fully accepted around the world!

To be effective, the global project management organization cannot be seen as being dominated by any one national organization. The association should be a federation of member national entities. One of the many challenges would be to determine how to establish voting rights in the federation. Would it be "one country, one vote" or would the voting be based on the size of the membership in any one country, or a combination of both? Regardless, the global project management association must be perceived as being "non-aligned" with any one country, otherwise it simply will not work.

Given the above, the mission of this global project management association needs to be stated in terms of service to member country organizations, and it should include such things as:

- Providing a vehicle for the establishment of a set of international project management standards that are endorsed by all member organizations
- Coordinating the use of project management resources around the world in carrying out special projects that are of interest and benefit to all member organizations
- Acting as an international spokesperson for the profession of project management
- Providing PMP certification guidelines to be used and modified by national organizations to reflect the unique requirements of any national jurisdiction
- Working to establish a universal project management classification system.

How can project management associations around the world better communicate and cooperate to advance the project management profession?

We have to become part of the "Information super highway" as a number one priority. With Internet and all of the wonderful innovations and changes that are occurring every day now, the world is truly shrinking. Our ability to come together, to meet, to discuss, and to make decisions is rapidly becoming economically possible. The cost of travel is no longer the dominant reason for keeping us apart.

YOUR ORGANIZATION

Briefly describe the history, purpose, organization and activities of the professional project management organization you represent.

PMI-Canada is a new organization with very little history but a great deal of future opportunities. PMI-Canada (which was officially formed with the signing of an inter-society co-operation agreement in May 1995) was created to address the unique needs of Canadian project management practitioners in Canada, and to foster the exchange of ideas and experience so as to:

- Advocate the growth of project management in Canada through the use of project management techniques and people
- Develop project management knowledge building and transfer
- Develop and adapt project management tools to the Canadian context
- Provide an identity for Canadian project management practitioners
- Provide project management career development and support
- Facilitate networking of project practitioners and Chapters.

Does your organization have established relations with agencies or departments of your government, or with universities? Please describe.

From PMI-Canada's perspective these relationships are either just in the formative stage (e.g., partnering arrangements are being established for the Calgary Seminar/Symposium) or are in the planning stage (e.g., the intent to establish close working relationships with engineering, architectural, medical, legal associations across Canada).

COLOMBIA

STATUS OF THE PROJECT MANAGEMENT PROFESSION

In general, at what stage is the project management profession in your country today (i.e., newly introduced, growing, mature)? Please comment.

The project management profession was introduced in Colombia by multinational companies, mainly related to the oil industry, more than ten years ago. Today, project management is growing steadily, but not as fast as we would like it.

There are a limited number of universities giving seminars and courses on project management. As a matter of fact, I have been teaching seminars in a local university (Universidad Javeriana de Cali) for five years now to more than 500 students. Also, consultancy in this field is very scarce, and my company is the only consulting company in Colombia with a specific contract to implement project management in a governmental institution. We have been working with the Utilities Company of Cali (EMCALI), telecommunications, energy, water and sewers, and public works, for more than a year in order to implement project management in this company, which is executing projects for about US $250 million per year. For this job we are using 100 percent, and quite successfully, the PMBOK approach.

What industries or types of projects are the main users of modern project management in your country or region today?

The main industries using modern project management are oil refining, pipelines, gas lines and the big chemical companies, especially the ones related to multinational companies.

What industries or areas of application in your country have the greatest need for more or better project management? What industries or organizations offer the greatest opportunities for growth of professional project management in your country? Why?

The utilities companies seem to have the greatest need for project management, because this sector, besides growing rapidly, is facing strong competition from the private sector due to the relatively recent privatization campaign initiated by the government. Also, the civil works construction companies should take a step in the project management direction since traditionally its approach has been one of only contract management, without consideration for other aspects of the project.

How can the project management profession be most effectively advanced in your country?

The formation of a local PMI chapter to promote project management education and project management application to important projects could be an important step forward.

What impact will globally recognized project management standards or certification have on the project management profession in your country?

They could help with the recognition of project management as an effective and safe way to execute projects.

ISSUES OF COMMON GLOBAL INTEREST

What should be contained in a global Project Management Body of Knowledge (PMBOK)?

I think a totally new integrated approach is needed since the excessive taxonomy implied in the actual PMBOK can be misleading to cultures that have a tendency to look at things in a more integrating and global way.

For this reason the following approach, which takes into consideration three big areas, could be a compromise between the two extremes: a fully integrated approach and a fully partitioned one. I am convinced by experience in my country that the following approach helps managers to focus on the main issues of the project and makes it easier for them to develop the required managerial skills.

Resource Management is the art and science of managing effectively all the resources required to execute the project. It includes:

- Human Resources Management—all the efforts needed to have, internally and externally, the required people with the suitable qualifications, working effectively and enthusiastically to reach the project objectives.
- Procurement—to provide in a timely fashion, with the defined quality level, all the equipment, materials, services and labor required to materialize the project.
- Communications—the establishment of the required infrastructure together with the development of appropriate skills to manage effectively all the project-related information, so that the project objectives can be achieved.

Plan Management is the art and science required to ensure the project objectives through analysis and prediction of all project-relevant aspects and monitoring and control of the subsequent plan. To successfully carry out the plan the following functions must be managed:

- Scope Management—the management of the extent or content of the job, which is described by identifying and naming all activities which must be executed, all final resulting products and the resources that must be used to execute the projects.
- Time Management—required to predict, organize and maintain the control of all time-related events in order to carry out the project in the span of time assigned to it by the owner.
- Cost Management—the execution of all required processes to maintain the financial control of the project in order to assure the timely availability of the assigned funds required to successfully complete the job.

Performance Management takes care of the project execution and the project itself as a product performs as planned and expected by the owner. It requires the execution of the following functions:

- Quality—this function must be regarded with the dual objective of accomplishing the project execution performance as regarded by the owner and stakeholders and the project fulfilling the established requirements as a product. In the first case, it must be sure that the project is executed according to the scope, time and cost objectives together with participants satisfaction. In the second case, it must take care of fulfilling all quality requirements of the project to operate as expected by the stakeholders.
- Risk Management—the art and science of identifying, analyzing and responding the risk factors that can negatively affect the project execution. Risk can be viewed as contrary to quality, according to the above definitions of both items.

How important will international "standards" for project management be in your country or region? Please comment.

They are essential for two reasons: It will help developing countries to improve their performance in project execution and also allow the globalization of a very important profession.

If they are adopted, project managers should be forced to follow them in their professional activities.

Is project management certification of interest in your country? What type of project management certification?

No response given.

What is your interest or position on a unified global project management association or organization? If you support such an organization, how should it be organized and for what objectives?

I think that a unified global project management association will be a giant step toward the development of the project management profession and through it, we can improve the welfare and development of all nations.

The organization must be a neutral one, i.e. not dominated by any country in particular, and it should consist of both membership of local organizations as well as individuals willing to help the project management profession advance. More than anything it should be the center of communications between the professionals of all the world and the entity in care of maintaining a homogeneous development of the project management profession.

How can project management associations around the world better communicate and cooperate to advance the project management profession?

I think there are two main channels to be maintained simultaneously: A global newspaper dedicated mainly to news and local issues that can be of interest to the international project management community, and the participation of all the associations around the world via the Internet.

YOUR ORGANIZATION

Briefly describe the history, purpose, organization and activities of the professional project management organization you represent.

A project management organization does not exist in Colombia. A few years ago I tried to promote one, but met with difficulties: I could only raise the amount of project management members from 4 to 17, and they were scattered all over the country.

For countries where the project management profession is not established, it could be helpful to allow national associations with members living in different cities until there is enough people to have a local association.

Does your organization have established relations with agencies or departments of your government, or with universities?

Not applicable.

CZECH REPUBLIC

STATUS OF THE PROJECT MANAGEMENT PROFESSION

In general, at what stage is the project management profession in your country today (i.e., newly introduced, growing, mature)? Please comment.

The project management profession is not recognized as a special one since the definition of a project is rather intuitive. Projects are not fully recognized and defined. They are mostly managed by functional managers as a part of their daily work.

What industries or types of projects are the main users of modern project management in your country or region today?

The main user of some project management methods and techniques is the construction industry. There is a quite long tradition in management of so-called investment projects. There used to be a specialized legislation in place providing construction delivery procedures based on network analysis.

No other industry or main specific user is known for utilizing generally accepted project management practices.

What industries or areas of application in your country have the greatest need for more or better project management? What industries or organizations offer the greatest opportunities for growth of professional project management in your country? Why?

The structure and volume of project management application could be the same and even wider as it is accepted in the highly developed industrial (and information) countries. Government (state and local), research and development groups and institutions, and new privately owned industrial companies and developer groups are in the greatest need. Large formerly state-owned industrial corporations are in need of redefining and establishing new project management practices. The major area of application appears to be information system integration.

The opportunities for professional growth in project management are very scarce. Small private mostly foreign consulting companies and internal training programs of large supranational firms provide some of the opportunities. Universities and general academic environments provide some of the theoretical aspects about project management methods and techniques.

> [Although] an interest in project management was established in the Czech Republic in 1967, there is no project management society [there] ... but I sense that there is a huge potential. We are a young, energetic country, and we are eager to learn from countries with established project management societies rather than starting from scratch ... why reinvent the wheel?
>
> Roman Chudoba, PMMS

How can the project management profession be most effectively advanced in your country?

The project management profession could be rapidly advanced by getting managers sensitized to project management concepts and approaches. The biggest gap is the knowledge and information. Consistent materials and training on project management should be available in Czech. The Project Management Society (SPPR) ought to be broadened and empowered.

What impact will globally recognized project management standards or certification have on the project management profession in your country?

Globally recognized project management standards could perform a crucial role in advancement of modern project management professional practice. It could provide a model, guidelines and basis for international collaboration on projects. Use of a commonly shared framework of reference could help gather and organize existing knowledge and experience and establish the basis for further development. Compliance with international quality standards would also be valuable.

ISSUES OF COMMON GLOBAL INTEREST

What should be contained in a global Project Management Body of Knowledge (PMBOK)?
- The key part should be dedicated to terms of reference, definitions and descriptions of generally accepted project management practices.
- In other parts there should be a systematic overview of project management methods, tools, techniques and ways of application.
- Case studies, checklists and general examples of documentation could be included.
- Multimedia appears to be the appropriate technology for storing and spreading the information.

How important will international "Standards" for project management be in your country or region? Please comment.

Since the Czech Republic is a small country and is an integral part of Europe, it has to closely collaborate with other countries; the more the better. International standards could increase the efficiency and effectiveness of bilateral and multilateral cooperation. The business volume between countries could be increased in both directions.

Education and training of project managers could be provided much more efficiently. Comparing national knowledge and experience bases against a broadly shared framework would be inspiring for all those involved.

Is project management certification of interest in your country? What type of project management certification?

Currently there is no need for project management certification. There is no demand for project management professionals. Thus no type of project management certification is requested. Certification might become an issue, but only if requested by an international organization.

What is your interest or position on a unified global project management association or organization? If you support such an organization, how should it be organized and for what objectives?

It is always a challenge to create something globally unifying. Such an organization could provide valuable services,and decrease costs. But it could turn into a bureaucratic body spending money of its members, building barriers to competition and curtailing creative change and further development.

The global organization shall serve as an information platform, gather information, initiate meetings and empower global contacts. It shall not certify, provide audits and accreditation. It should empower national members to do so by providing information, facilitating professional discussions and creating an appropriate image. Basically it shall not be involved in any regulating practices. It shall be easily accessible at a low cost.

How can project management associations around the world better communicate and cooperate to advance the project management profession?

The crucial need is for information technology. Use of the Internet or other international information networks is a necessity. However, the point of personal contact should be at least in each country. This point could closely collaborate with a national project management organization, but in terms of budget and operations should be 100 percent responsible to the "global body."

YOUR ORGANIZATION

Briefly describe the history, purpose, organization and activities of the professional project management organization you represent.

Project Management Society (Spolecnost pro projektove reizeni - SPPR) was established in 1990. The society was created from the Internet (now IMPA) National Committee that was established in the spring of 1989 as a part of the Czech Society for Science and Technology. Before the political changes in the country it was very difficult to organize such an activity internationally. however, a Czech specialist, as an individual, used to collaborate with Internet since it was established in 1967.

Currently SPPR has 37 individual (7 women) and 5 corporate members. Most of the active members are academically oriented university teachers.

Since the project management profession is not widely recognized, the membership base is small; the budget for one year is about $3,000.

During the last few years SPPR organized seminars (3–5 a year). The last seminar was held in 1994 utilizing open space technology. The seminar was organized and facilitated by one of the corporate members: private project management consulting company. In September 1995 the first regional congress on project management is going to be held.

Currently SPPR is redirecting its strategy toward:
- Points of professional contacts
- Building project management know-how fund, nationalize PMBOK
- Fostering project management understanding
- Certification and accreditation.

Does your organization have established relations with agencies or departments of your government, or with universities? Please describe.

SPPR has a very close relationship with universities since 35 percent of the members are university teachers and students. Relations with government departments is very vague, and SPPR has no practical impact. There are no working relations with other agencies.

EGYPT

STATUS OF THE PROJECT MANAGEMENT PROFESSION

In general, at what stage is the project management profession in your country today (i.e., newly introduced, growing, mature?)

The project management profession is growing in Egypt. It started in the late '70s but is limited in its applications to "hard" project engineering-procurement-installation.

What industries or types of projects are the main users of modern project management in your country or region today?

Its main users in Egypt are the petroleum-related industries, followed by the electricity sector, large water and waste water projects, infrastructure, civil and industrial projects.

What industries or areas of application in your country have the greatest need for more or better project management? What industries or organizations offer the greatest opportunities for growth of professional project management in your country? Why?

All industries are in need of better project management.

How can the project management profession be most effectively advanced in your country?

Project management can only be effectively advanced when accountability is applied to the project manager.

What impact will globally recognized project management standards or certification have on the project management profession in your country?

It will enhance the profession.

> Egypt has a long history of project management, going back to the project of the pyramids ... it's interesting to note that that the first letters of the project management concepts Responsibility, Accountability, and Authority spell out the name of the ancient Egyptian god of gods, Raa, the Creator... Today, in new industries, we must apply project management to managing the creative process.
>
> Ahmed Seif El Din, MES

ISSUES OF COMMON GLOBAL INTEREST

What should be contained in a global Project Management Body of Knowledge (PMBOK)?

This will need a separate and detailed response.

How important will international "Standards" be for project management in your country or region? Please comment.

Each project is unique and each manager is unique, each contract, each owner or owner's representative ... are unique, so we need "unique standards."

Is project management certification of interest in your country? What type of project management certification?

Certification is important and of interest.

What is your interest or position on a unified global project management association or organization? If you support such an organization, how should it be organized and for what objectives?

We need a global project management association with a strong technical alliance and weak interference in regional turfs. Let's not step on toes. Its objectives should be:

- Further development of the PMBOK (the PMI BOK, APM, GPM, IPMA, and any other regional BOKs)
- Balancing project manager Responsibility, Authority, and Accountability—RAA (the God of Gods in ancient Egypt)
- Project management contracts language—standard formats with different options: i.e., between client and project management firm or project manager; between project management firm and project manager
- Certification
- Standards (unique—maybe "guidelines" is more appropriate)
- Ensuring projects meet stakeholders' needs
- Project audit guidelines
- Project evaluation guidelines at go/no-go decision points and at completion.

How can project management associations around the world better communicate and cooperate to advance the project management profession?

As soon as the objectives are agreed upon in the global meetings held at PMI, IPMA, and elsewhere, cooperation and communication can be worked out.

YOUR ORGANIZATION

Briefly describe the history, purpose organization and activities of the professional project management organization you represent.

Omar Seif Elding & Sons is a private consulting firm, and is not the project management association in Egypt.

FRANCE

STATUS OF THE PROJECT MANAGEMENT PROFESSION

In general, at what stage is the project management profession in your country today (i.e., newly introduced, growing, mature)? Please comment.

Mature.

What industries or types of projects are the main users of modern project management in your country or region today?

Generally speaking, the majority of modern project management users belong to the following industries and are members of our association:
- Oil, gas, nuclear engineering
- Space, aeronautical industry
- Military engineering
- Iron and steel industry
- Car industry
- Pharmaceutical and chemical industry
- Shipbuilding industry
- Electronic/telecommunication
- Banking/insurance
- Services
- Manufacturing industries

> Speaking on behalf of AFITEP—which has 900 members and has published many books on project management—and of the PMI Chapter in France ... I take advantage of this opportunity to invite you all to attend the World Congress in Paris in June 1996.
>
> Michel Brix, PMI-France

What industries or areas of application in your country have the greatest need for more or better project management? What industries or organizations offer the greatest opportunities for growth of professional project management in your country? Why?

No comment.

How can the project management profession be most effectively advanced in your country?

No comment.

What impact will globally recognized project management standards or certification have on the project management profession in your country?

No comment.

ISSUES OF COMMON GLOBAL INTEREST

What should be contained in a global Project Management Body of Knowledge (PMBOK)?

The main objectives of a PMBOK is to explain how to manage "the project" and it should contain at the minimum the following sections:
- Management of the project process
- Management of the design process
- Management of the procurement process
- Management of the construction process
- Management of the commissioning process
- Management of the quality of the product.

Each of the above subjects should incorporate PDCA (Plan, Do, Check, Analyze).

How important will international "Standards" for project management be in your country or region? Please comment.

International standards should reflect the needs of the profession.

ISO 9000 Bases

ISO 10000.6 Quality in Project Management.

It should be validated by different types of industries: i.e., International and U.S. Engineering.

Is project management certification of interest in your country? What type of project management certification?

Yes.

Since 1990, AFITEP has implemented an operational certification program (CMP: Certificat en Management de Projet).

Up to now, about 400 people have been certified and 150 more people have started the certification this year.

The present certification syllabus is split into 3 phases:

1. Justification of 3 to 7 years experience according to the obtained university degree
2. Four exams: 1/2 each on the following subjects:
   - Elements of project management
   - Estimating
   - Cost control
   - Planning/scheduling
3. Presentation of a paper on any of the above subjects.

Note: this certification is recognized by ICEC.

AFITEP is currently working on a project management Certification Program (C.D.P. = Certification des Directeurs de Projets), which will be operational in about a year.

What is your interest or position on a unified global project management association or organization? If you support such an organization, how should it be organized and for what objectives?

Countries that have well-established project management organizations could assist in setting up new associations in countries where this subject is not yet developed.

AFITEP is not in favor of a single unified global project management association across the world. In our opinion, the best results are obtained where the country creates its own project management organization. The public at large is positive to this policy. In the long term, it is more productive to "create" rather than to "receive."

AFITEP favors the creation of an international link between all project management associations.

How can project management associations around the world better communicate and cooperate to advance the project management profession?

An "umbrella" association should be created to formalize relations and maintain regular communications and cooperation among national associations. ICEC and IPMA are good examples of successful umbrella associations.

YOUR ORGANIZATION

Briefly describe the history, purpose, organization and activities of the professional project management organization you represent.

AFITEP (French Association of Project Management)
- Was created in 1982
- Was at first project control oriented
- Is now project control and project management oriented
- Has 900 full paying members
- Publishes a magazine *La Cible* (every two months)
- Has initiated the publication of books on project control and project management; a total of about 26 books have been published so far on the above subject and are the basis of our certification programs
- Has created and maintains a successful certification program (see "Is project management certification of interest …")
- Is currently developing another certification program on project management (see "Is project management certification of interest …")
- Maintains strong links with IPMA; the French branch of IPMA has merged with AFITEP
- Is organizing in 1996 an International Project Management Congress on behalf of IPMA.

Does your organization have established relations with agencies or departments of your government, or with universities? Please describe.

AFITEP acts in an advisory capacity to commissions headed by the French Department of Industry.

AFITEP participates in the commissions organized by AFNOR (AFNOR = Association française de Normalisation). AFNOR is the official French representative within the ISO technical committee.

AFITEP maintains healthy relations with universities and specialized schools involved in the certification program.

The AFITEP Board of Directors and the Certification Committees both include well-known academics in their memberships.

GERMANY

STATUS OF THE PROJECT MANAGEMENT PROFESSION

In general, at what stage is the project management profession in your country today (i.e., newly introduced, growing, mature)? Please comment.

No comment.

What industries or types of projects are the main users of modern project management in your country or region today?

No comment

What industries or areas of application in your country have the greatest need for more or better project management? What industries or organizations offer the greatest opportunities for growth of professional project management in your country? Why?

The project management profession is successfully introduced in civil and industrial engineering, pharmaceutical research and development, urban projects, housing, and ship building. The project management profession is newly introduced and growing in public administration and small- and medium-sized enterprises.

How can the project management profession be most effectively advanced in your country?

No comment.

What impact will globally recognized project management standards or certification have on the project management profession in your country?

GPM (Deutsche Gesellschaft für Projektmanagement) and associated organizations offer more than 20 long- and short-term courses and seminars per year, some of them with official certification. GPM offers a German and English library of new project management literature and publications.

There is a long-term training course (150 hours) with an official certificate, "PM Fachmann," which has had about 100 successful participants in the past three years. An equivalent training course was started for "PM Kauffmann."

The IPMA Certification Program is already implemented.

GPM Corporate Members are asking increasingly for in-house training courses with specific examination/certification.

> ● ● ● ● ● ● ● ● ● ●
>
> I'm a son of the father and following in his footsteps whenever I can, because I believe that project management is the profession of the future... The chief project management organization was founded in Germany the year I was born, so it is 28 years old. ...Today, in Germany, we need to reorganize all our organizations in a project management-related way....
>
> ● ● ● ● ● ● ● ● ● ●
>
> Olaf Pannenbäcker, GPM

ISSUES OF COMMON GLOBAL INTEREST

What should be contained in a global Project Management Body of Knowledge (PMBOK)?

GPM is evaluating all existing versions of project management bodies of knowledge, for developing a PMBOK with German project management understanding, together with SPM in Switzerland. Our experts do not expect only one overall PMBOK covering all branches, project management elements and phases under specific cultural aspects.

How important will international "Standards" for project management be in your country or region? Please comment.

Especially globally active companies have a strong demand for training their managers in project management competencies under specific cultural requirements.

Is project management certification of interest in your country? What type of project management certification?

See "What industries or areas of application…" above.

What is your interest or position on a unified global project management association or organization? If you support such an organization, how should it be organized and for what objectives?

GPM agrees on a unified global project management understanding, but does not promote a global project management organizational body. The existing national associations are responsible for their own activities, and globalization is based only on a unification of the PMBOK, that is, project management certification with international accreditation.

How can project management associations around the world better communicate and cooperate to advance the project management profession?

All umbrella organizations (IPMA, PMI, AIPM, etc.) will have to start with working groups for project management products and services. For practical matters, the exchange of addresses and invitations for events is evident.

YOUR ORGANIZATION

Briefly describe the history, purpose, organization and activities of the professional project management organization you represent.

GPM has about 1,100 members including approximately 100 corporate members and 60 students.

GPM has a Board of eight members, a secretariat with three employees and more than 20 regional representatives.

For the past 6 years, GPM has installed regional groups which are responsible for local member meetings. In addition, there are several specific groups dealing with project management development in different branches on an interdisciplinary basis. All groups are run independently, as so-called Competence Centres.

In addition to a quarterly distributed magazine, *GPM-aktuell*, GPM publishes a common *Journal of Project Management* together with SPM in Switzerland and PMA in Austria.

Does your organization have established relations with agencies or departments of your government, or with universities? Please describe.

GPM is in cooperation with major non-profit organizations in Germany for research in project management as well as for project management promotion in general. Several cooperating universities run project management education programs.

There are several cooperation projects co-financed by industry and government.

GREECE

STATUS OF THE PROJECT MANAGEMENT PROFESSION

In general, at what stage is the project management profession in your country today (i.e., newly introduced, growing, mature)? Please comment.

Project management in Greece is a relatively new profession, but as a concept it has been well known in our country for quite some time. Nevertheless, we have recently observed a great interest towards project management. This growing interest in project management has, at least in part, resulted from the fact that the European Commission is currently requiring it for the supervision (according to established project management techniques) of all major Support Framework (Delar's II) financed projects. Due to the fact that these specific contracts allot considerable budgets for project management (1,500,000 ECU – 15,000,000 ECU) and, since there is a lack of similar experience in Greece, these projects are likely to be assigned to large companies from the USA, England, Germany, France, etc. Nevertheless, Greek companies and professionals will be included in the consortiums undertaking such projects and will therefore gain further practical experience. Given these activities, there will be a boost in the Greek project management field.

What industries or types of projects are the main users of modern project management in your country or region today?

Project management activities in Greece are expected to mainly involve large technical project such as:
- Motorways
- Railways
- Airways
- Ports
- Gas pipelines, etc.

What industries or areas of application in your country have the greatest need for more or better project management? What industries or organizations offer the greatest opportunities for growth of professional project management in your country? Why?

In the industrial sector, project management techniques/methodologies are rarely practiced in Greece. Nevertheless, I believe that the expected large increase in the number of technical projects will influence project management's development in this sector.

How can the project management profession be most effectively advanced in your country?

To date, interest in project management has been almost exclusively limited to the training of engineers. I believe that the training in project management techniques will

contribute to the improvement of the project management profession, and that this training should occur in two areas:
1. Through the universities, as a specialization or as a post-graduate degree
2. At a professional level, as specialized seminars for the training of professionals who undertake projects and who wish to improve their knowledge of project management.

What impact will globally recognized project management standards or certification have on the project management profession in your country?

"Global Standards" are necessary in all sectors, and of course project management is no exception. As a small country, without significant industrial development, Greece has suffered from the lack of standardization. However, the fact that Greeks are acutely aware of this problem suggests that steps will be taken toward achieving international standards for project management. In any case, now that the economy is internationalized, the internationalization of standards is crucial.

ISSUES OF COMMON GLOBAL INTEREST

What should be contained in a global Project Management Body of Knowledge (PMBOK)?

No comments.

How important will international "Standards" for project management be in your country or region? Please comment.

See "What impact will globally recognized ..." above.

Is project management certification of interest in your country? What type of project management certification?

Project management certification is of great interest for our country. I believe that this certification should take place at both the individual level as well as at the company level, according to ISO 9000.

What is your interest or position on a unified global project management association or organization? If you support such an organization, how should it be organized and for what objectives?

A unified global project management association could enhance the rapid transfer of information concerning new developments and methodologies, as well as promote reasonable standards for project management professionals/ companies.

How can project management associations around the world better communicate and cooperate to advance the project management profession?

Based on the fact that our association is very young and has limited experience, concerning matters such as the organization and communication of project management associations, I prefer to leave these remarks to other European colleagues who benefit from more experience.

YOUR ORGANIZATION

Briefly describe the history, purpose, organization and activities of the professional project management organization you represent.

The HPMI was founded in 1992 in response to the need for an institutional framework that would embrace the advancement of project management in Greece. It operates as a resource pool and provides a platform from which to exchange experiences and discuss problems as well as a locus for members to keep abreast of new systems and international developments affecting project management applications, trends and methodologies.

The HPMI is a non-profit and independent professional organization committed to representing the professional interests of its members and enhancing technical standards.

The HPMI provides the following activities and services:
- Information services, including regular newsletters giving updates on the field
- Specialist journals, which are circulated to the members
- Seminar proceedings, books and publications available to members at a discount
- Computerized databank of project management literature and events
- Annual directory of members, listing individuals and companies active in project management
- International Project Management Association Membership.

Does your organization have established relations with agencies or departments of your government, or with universities? Please describe.

HPMI operates mainly on a network basis, with access to several organizations, professionals and academics in several European and Third World countries. Although relations with government bodies and universities are mainly of an informal nature, HPMI counts on close relations/support of several Greek universities and public institutes.

INDIA

STATUS OF THE PROJECT MANAGEMENT PROFESSION

In general, at what stage is the project management profession in your country today (i.e., newly introduced, growing, mature)? Please comment.

India is a mixed economy, almost equal balance between government and privately owned enterprises. It is dominated by an agricultural economy in co-existence with industrial to information technology age economies. India is currently undergoing a massive transformation phase to integrate with the global economy. The economic reforms in India are irreversible.

The project management profession in India exhibits a highly varied picture. Whereas large projects adopt sophisticated project management methodology, medium projects use simple planning techniques. The project management profession is at a growing stage, displaying a tremendous potential for growth.

What industries or types of projects are the main users of modern project management in your country or region today?

Project Management Associates (PMA) supports the views of the Center for Excellence in Project Management in dividing projects into "hard" and "soft" sectors. While hard projects relate to construction activities, installation of new production lines, and complex aerospace/defense projects, soft projects relate to organizational or cultural change, human network aspects, and total quality management, etc. In almost all hard sector projects, project management techniques are now being used. The importance of using project management techniques is being realized for soft projects related to education, health, and poverty alleviation programs.

Project management techniques are used in all internationally funded projects financed by The World Bank, Asian Development Bank, etc.

> The world has become a family ... we are the first generation of global citizens. In India we see the coexistence of three historical types of economies—agricultural, industrial, and information—side by side. Change is going at such an accelerated pace that we don't know what will happen to us and it is in this field of change management that project management has to play a superhero role .... in the "soft sector" of organizational and cultural change projects.
>
> Adesh Jain, PMA

What industries or areas of application in your country have the greatest need for more or better project management? What industries or organizations offer the greatest opportunities for growth of professional project management in your country? Why?

Almost across all sectors in both hard and soft projects. Infrastructure construction projects covering transportation, utility, telecommunication and housing will be the greatest beneficiaries.

How can the project management profession be most effectively advanced in your country?

The following nine steps are suggested.
1. Follow life cycle phases to project management.
2. Put greater emphasis on project planning and conceptualization.
3. Do "What if" analysis for various combinations of scenarios. This would reduce unexpected outcomes during the execution phase.
4. Empower people to get out of grooves, explore new things, bestow faith and trust in colleagues, see "whole" and not "parts," proactive in change management and provide larger meaning to one's life.
5. Establish sustainable values and attitudes.
6. Understand in clear terms the immense potential of motivating individuals and teams for higher productivity and lower conflicts and more focus on customers at all times.
7. Establish certificate programs leading to the award of project management diploma/certificate.
8. Strengthen national project management associations.
9. Take no short cuts. Quality should become the hallmark of our actions.

What impact will globally recognized project management standards or certification have on the project management profession in your country?

A great deal.

In today's borderless world, the integration of diversified cultures and different economic positioning is forcing companies to increasingly use project management techniques to maintain a lead in the marketplace. While we adopt and fine-tune to global experience and standards in project management, it is imperative that some modifications be made to suit specific requirements.

ISSUES OF COMMON GLOBAL INTEREST

What should be contained in a global Project Management Body of Knowledge (PMBOK)?

PMBOK should be specifically divided into two major parts, i.e., technical and behavioral planes. While the contents of the technical PMBOK may be applicable across nations and regions, there may be some variations in the behavioral plane.

In the technical plane, we can include topics covering Time Management, Scope Management, Contract Management, Cost Management, Risk Management, Quality Management, Planning and Control Mechanisms, Information Technology, and Office Automation.

In the behavioral plane, we could provide coverage of Conflict Resolution Mechanism, Communication, Team Building Processes, Role of Leadership, Philosophy of Sustainability, Customer Orientation, and Human Network Management.

How important will international "Standards" for project management be in your country or region? Please comment.

Standards are welcome to the extent that they should not stifle innovation and creativity. A proper balance is to be struck between standards and flexibility. This balance, in our opinion, would be a critical element in the success of global standards. Flexibility must be built by providing user-friendly entry and exit points from various standards.

Is project management certification of interest in your country? What type of project management certification?

Yes. Because the project management discipline is in the growth stage, a certification program is desirable to provide continuing updating of skills to practicing project managers. In developing countries, a certification program will be more relevant because it will help in catching up with the rest of the world. It will also provide easy operability to transnational corporations when expanding their operations in developing economies.

What is your interest or position on a unified global project management association or organization? If you support such an organization, how should it be organized and for what objectives?

We see merit in the unification of global project management associations. The world is becoming more integrated and, thanks to technology, economic compulsions, and the opening up of the people's desire to seek more meaning to their lives, there is a tremendous scope to unifying efforts of national project management associations.

We are perhaps the first generation of global citizens and it is in this light that we have to address the question of unification of project management associations. Speeding up this unification process of project management associations will provide a better integration among countries and companies. This would facilitate managing change effectively.

Project management is a way of thinking. It is a way of working, irrespective of the type of work. Extensive experience sharing will become an important aspect in moving into the 21st century. Global project management associations can provide an effective platform for experience sharing.

In terms of organization structure for a global project management association, we see a danger of it becoming bureaucratic. An innovative approach to organization structure for such a global body is a must. It should have an apex body of elected representatives, with different fields of specialization and with regional operations divided into three major regions, i.e., North and South America, Europe, and Asia-Pacific. A global project management association should be organized on the sound principles of business followed by international companies.

A responsive organization structure enabling speedy communication should be the basis of its creation.

How can project management associations around the world better communicate and cooperate to advance the project management profession?

Project management associations should cooperate to advance the project management profession through better inter-connectivity to ensure better response time amongst the various project management associations. Some of the suggested steps are:

- Be connected through e-mail
- Meet on a regular basis, say once every six months
- Share experiences and research work in the area of project management
- Support in framing project management standards
- Have a regular publication highlighting case studies
- Create a publication center reflecting viewpoints of national associations
- Allow publication of articles across the journals and magazines of various associations, with due acknowledgment.

YOUR ORGANIZATION

Briefly describe the history, purpose, organization and activities of the professional project management organization you represent.

Project Management Associates (PMA) is a registered not-for-profit society dedicated to the cause of spreading project management principles. It has supported the definition of Center for Excellence in Project Management in defining project management where "project" means mission and "management" means efficient and effective accomplishment.

It came into being in July 1993. To our knowledge, this is the only registered body representing the interest of project management professionals in India.

It has an Executive Committee (EC) composed of 8 members. The EC elects the president, vice president and treasurer. Mr. Adesh Jain is the elected honorary president for the 3 year period until 1996. He is also eligible for re-election after the expiry of the term.

PMA has now completed its business plans. In the next 12 months, PMA has targeted to enroll 100 individual members and 50 organizational members. The growth of PMA is anticipated to be between 30 to 40 percent in terms of increase in membership for the next four years.

Does your organization have established relations with agencies or departments of your government, or with universities? Please describe.

Yes, PMA has a strong link with the government and organizes various programs in association with the government. PMA was successful in organizing four major events in association with the government; namely, the Department of Public Enterprises and the Department of Program Implementation. The Department of Program Implementation is the key government department responsible for the planning and execution of all mega-projects in India.

PMA is also linked with prestigious institutions such as Indian Institute of Technology, Delhi. At present, the relationship is more dotted line and we hope to concretize this.

INDONESIA

STATUS OF THE PROJECT MANAGEMENT PROFESSION

In general, at what stage is the project management profession in your country today (i.e., newly introduced, growing, mature)? Please comment.

In the last two decades, the project management practice has been growing very rapidly in response to the rapid economic development of the country. However, its growth was not accompanied by the development of project management as an important profession. There were still no concerted efforts on the part of public, private sector, or of education institutions to organize the growth of project management practices into a more proper professional development. Therefore, we have observed that the role and impact of the project management profession in national development is not publicly recognized.

What industries or types of projects are the main users of modern project management in your country or region today?

In the public sector, the main users are public works department (highways, toll road related projects, water resources, water supply and sanitation projects); communication department (land, sea and air transportation projects); telecommunication and tourism department (telecommunication projects; tourism area destination infrastructure and facilities projects); energy department (electric power generation projects); and trade and industry department (industrial estate and industrial related projects). In the private sector, the main users are real estate and property developers, and industrial estates developers. In the last ten years we have seen private sector involvement in a variety of public-private arrangements (domestic as well as foreign): the construction of new towns, public infrastructure and facilities (electric power generation plants, energy related projects, toll road projects, airport projects).

> A lot of Indonesian companies are assisted by foreign project managers, but there is little communication about project management within Indonesia, although there are several PMI members... my goal is to translate the *PMBOK Guide* into Indonesian language.
>
> John Tjahjadi, PMI

What industries or areas of application in your country have the greatest need for more or better project management? What industries or organizations offer the greatest opportunities for growth of professional project management? Why?

The greatest need for better project management is in the public infrastructure and utilities construction sector (road projects, water supply and environmental sanitation projects, energy projects etc.). This is not only because of its important role in the national development, but also because these subsectors show a substantial backlog. Experience shows that there is a need to focus more on the quality of public infrastructure construction, such as the improvement of inspection system, optimization of system components etc. (see World Bank, Indonesia Public Infrastructure Services, 1993).

In order to develop this profession effectively, the importance of professional project management in national development must be recognized and properly placed in national policy-related documents or regulations. There are three channels that may promote opportunities for the growth of the project management profession. The first is through Bappenas (National Development Planning Board), the central government agency that is responsible for infrastructure construction projects. Bappenas must recognize the need and benefits of developing, organizing and enhancing the project management profession for national development. The second channel is through the international lending and financial institutions such as the World Bank, Asian Development Bank, UNDP, Citibank, etc. where these institutions have been providing great contribution to the development of strategic projects in the country. These agencies may require the use of project management qualifications, techniques for all of their funded projects. The third channel is through international companies such as AT&T and ABB, which already implement project management techniques in their projects elsewhere, to support similar practices in Indonesia. I think that only with these three channels can the impact of this profession be greatly appreciated.

How can the project management profession be most effectively advanced in your country?

The project management profession was not well developed in Indonesia because of the lack of a systematic, comprehensive approach in its development. To effectively develop, besides the approach suggested above (thorough cooperation with Bappenas and international lending agencies) there is need to establish a national association that will be responsible for organizing, regulating, providing technical assistance in education and training for project management professionals to attain a recognized project management qualification. The role of PMI in this process is very important. The organizational arrangements of the national association can be PMI chapter or joint cooperation with PMI.

What impact will globally recognized project management standards or certification have on the project management profession in your country?

Since the economy of the country is becoming more global, the use of internationally recognized project management certification and standards are becoming more needed to be able to compete in the global market. The impact will be (1) to enhance the credibility of project management profession; (2) to have better qualification of project management professionals (3) to have better monitoring, control and technical assistance of professional growth and development; (4) to have better quality project completion.

ISSUES OF COMMON GLOBAL INTEREST

What should be contained in a global Project Management Body of Knowledge (PMBOK)?

It is very important the PMBOK contain
- a model national policy statement that can be adopted by developing countries such as Indonesia, describing the background, roles and importance (rationale) of

this profession in achieving the national development objectives
- the benefits that can be gained from such professional development
- a systematic approach for developing and strengthening the profession
- the role and responsibilities of government, private sector, communities, educational institutions and international lending agencies in its development
- a model action plan that can be followed.

How important will international "Standards" for project management be in your country or region? Please comment?

The degree of importance of such international standards will vary according to type, scale, public or private, policy of government, funding sources, beneficiaries of the project.

Is the project management certification of interest in your country? What type of project management certification?

Yes, of great interest. All levels of project management certification will be welcome.

What is your interest or position on a unified global project management association or organization? If you support such an organization, how should it be organized and for what objectives?

It would be beneficial if, in the immediate future, PMI could provide technical assistance to develop such a proposal (blue print) for the development of project management profession in Indonesia. A policy paper should be submitted and disseminated to relevant government agencies and actors involved in project management providing a comprehensive overview of roles and importance of this profession, benefits accrued, roles and responsibilities of public, private, communities in this development, organizational arrangements etc. The objectives of such a document would be to disseminate better understanding of the profession; to facilitate systematic professional development; and most importantly, to have better impact on national development.

To effectively disseminate it, the organization that cooperates with PMI in preparing the documents, must consist of individuals from all sectors, government agencies, private and communities, peers and media. It would be good if such activities could be funded through international associations, or organizations in donor countries and sources generated locally.

How can project management associations around the world better communicate and cooperate to advance the project management profession?

There is need to have regular regional seminars or workshops (developed on sustainable basis) conducted yearly focusing on different aspects of project management; and a newsletter/bulletin that informs on the latest development of the profession and practices.

YOUR ORGANIZATION

Briefly describe the history, purpose, organization and activities of the professional project management organization you represent.

P.T. Dacrea is a wholly private company established in 1974. The purpose is to provide the public and private sectors a wide range of consultancy services in the field or architecture, engineering and planning, including project construction supervision and project construction management. Since its establishment, P.T. Dacrea has been involved in a substantial number of strategic government as well as private projects in the country. The major projects are design, construction supervision of public infrastructure and utilities (such as road and water supply projects) and construction management of substantial number of leading private projects in the building, property development. Recently P.T. Dacrea PM, a subsidiary of P.T. Dacrea, obtained Certificate of Quality Management System ISO 9001 in the area of design and construction management.

Does your organization have established relations with agencies or departments of your government, or with universities?

Yes, we have established relations with almost all important government agencies, central government as well as local government; and also government owned companies. Relations with university is established on a project basis.

IRELAND

STATUS OF THE PROJECT MANAGEMENT PROFESSION

In general, at what stage is the project management profession in your country today (i.e., newly introduced, growing, mature)? Please comment.

Project management in Ireland today would be in an early growth phase. It would not be formally recognized as a profession but rather as a complementary skills set to an existing professional qualification such as engineering, accounting, marketing.

Organizations, save perhaps for construction and information technology, would seldom advertise exclusively for a project manager. However, there is a growing recognition of and requirement for middle and senior management to also have project management skills in many functional organizations.

What industries or types of projects are the main users of modern project management in your country or region today?

Project management would be firmly rooted in both the construction and information technology industries, as alluded to above. Within these industries, especially in the construction sector, project management would not necessarily be practiced across the entire life cycle but would have a greater weighting to the implementation phase. This is changing as clients are becoming more discerning and knowledgeable.

What industries or areas of application in your country have the greatest need for more or better project management? What industries or organizations offer the greatest opportunities for growth of professional project management in your country? Why?

The majority of organizations we encounter are functional. There is a definite need in these organizations for project management to fill in the gaps between the functions when tackling projects—the requirement for "total perspective" to be maintained.

These organizations spread across many industry sectors:
- State
- Semi-State
- Financial Services
- Manufacturing.

As so many organizations are encountering major changes (e.g., the semi-state sectors facing new liberalization and anti-monopoly legislation) the *requirement* for a "projects office" approach to plan, prioritize, and coordinate projects and resources is a significant growth opportunity for project management. The trick here is to create the awareness of and understanding of the benefits of such an approach to the executive management.

How can the project management profession be most effectively advanced in your country?

The project management profession can be most effectively advanced by offering interested parties a focal point such as our own national organization in conjunction with a strong infrastructural backup support from a body such as PMI. We are a small country, approximating in size and population to Washington State in the U.S., and we believe that PMI has both the size, backup and global vision to allow us to develop without having to reinvent the wheel.

What impact will globally recognized project management standards or certification have on the project management profession in your country?

We believe that a globally recognized project management certification will enhance the interest of people in bolting-on such a recognition to their primary professional degree. There is a demand on our young, educated workforce to be much more internationally mobile than before, especially in the context of our role within the European Community. A globally recognized certification will lead to greater marketability and shift acceptance of its validity in multinational companies and across national boundaries.

ISSUES OF COMMON GLOBAL INTEREST

We wish to preface our comments by stating that because of our size and the fact that the profession is in an early growth phase here, our concentration has been primarily on domestic development.

What should be contained in a global Project Management Body of Knowledge (PMBOK)?

We would be familiar with both APM BOK and PMI BOK. We believe that an executive overview might be appropriate in order to provide potential users with a simplified mental picture as to what it is all about. This overview might also reflect a relative weighting of importance to each module. For example, one has no relativity measures within the PMI BOK modules other than "core and enabling." Our experiences have been that the "enabling" modules, which include both Human Resources and Communications, are frequently the most difficult ground to manage in Modern Project Management. The suggested format of this overview might be:

- Global Issues (big picture)
- Hard Issues (quantitative)
- Soft Issues (people).

This could be presented on a single A4 page exploded out into a WBS format. People involved in project management are operating at different levels and different zones. We have found that by presenting project management in such a manner that they appreciate its totality and recognize where they are currently operating.

How important will international "Standards" for project management be in your country or region? Please comment.

We do not believe that international "standards" are a significant issue at the present time. This is due to the early growth stage that project management is currently at here.

However, we are of the opinion that this situation will change in the short term as European Union harmonization progresses and U.S. and other multinational organizations seek consistency and uniformity in their satellite organizations' approach to project management. International standards aligned with recognized certifications will render project management a very attractive option.

Is project management certification of interest in your country? What type of project management certification?

Certification is of considerable interest in our country. The first form of recognition/certification looked for is a formal body to certify educational/training programs undertaken. This is viewed primarily as an academic qualification to enable the individual to be more marketable within their company and/or in the employment marketplace. Certification as a PMP, for example, is now being considered under two categories. One option is to look outward to a body such as PMI or IPMA. The other option is the development of a national certification program. We in the Institute favor the former; we are not convinced there is a sufficient demand in the country to justify otherwise. The latter option would be the favored approach of some academics and particularly engineers who are interested in representing project management as a subset group of their professional body.

What is your interest or position on a unified global project management association or organization? If you support such an organization, how should it be organized and for what objectives?

We believe that national organizations will likely wish to maintain some form of identity that will appeal to their indigenous membership. We support the concept of a unified global project management association that will accommodate these cultural considerations. Such an entity should be an umbrella organization with a strong infra-structural base capable of supporting the needs of the member bodies and associations. It should also work toward the development of universal standards, accreditation and certification criteria.

How can project management associations around the world better communicate and cooperate to advance the project management profession?

Project management associations around the world can communicate and cooperate through people, journals and technology. Whenever I have attended a PMI conference my primary interest was in meeting people and finding out "what is new/what is happening—has it any relevance to the environment that I live in." As such, we strongly endorse opportunities such as a PMI '95 Global Project Management Forum, which will enable swift dissemination of current information and exchange of ideas through personal contact.

Our primary journal materials are *International Journal of Project Management and PM Network*. Both journals offer quality materials that help us to keep abreast of current developments. We find that *PM Network* provides a more vibrant and lively presentation format.

From a technology perspective we believe that the best opportunities to communicate are through the Internet medium. We recently tried to access PMI through this medium but the information available was limited. We were interested to see if information was available on all PMI publications so that we might zone in on particular topics. We were unable to do so. We did access the WWW Project Management Forum and found that the proposed structure and current status of information was of great interest. This medium offers a quick and cost-effective mechanism for global communication, which also enables excellent cooperation between interested bodies.

YOUR ORGANIZATION

Briefly describe the history, purpose, organization and activities of the professional project management organization you represent.

The Institute of Project Management (Ireland) was founded in 1989. Many professional societies had attempted to serve this need through the creation of sections, divisions, or special interest groups. These efforts did not fulfill the need of specialists in the field. For these reasons an Irish organization devoted solely to project management was formed.

The principal objectives are to:
- Promote the "management by projects" approach to service the challenges facing business.
- Create an environment in which project management techniques and experiences can be developed and shared.
- Offer guidance for instruction and career development in project management.
- Encourage the application of project management skills to a diverse range of disciplines and provide training in project management development.

The activities include symposia, seminars, workshops, lectures and publications of papers in professional journals, which are all geared to heighten the awareness and promote interest in project management. For example, the symposia we organize tend to be done in conjunction with high-profile organizations that have recently undertaken very visible and well-known projects. This provides credibility to the topic of project management, attracts a wider audience, and introduces many people to the opportunities and benefits that project management can bring to their own organization.

Does your organization have established relations with agencies or departments of your government, or with universities? Please describe.

Our organization does not have any established links with agencies or departments of government at this time. This would be primarily due to our small size and a reflection of the current status of project management in the country. However, many government departments and most of the semi-state companies that are very large employers would definitely be aware of our existence.

The National University of Ireland is composed of three separate universities spread geographically throughout the country. We have entered into an arrangement with one of these—University College Cork, Dept.. of Management and Marketing—whereby we run a joint program titled the "diploma in applied project management." University College Cork is 150 years old and has a student population of 10,000. We are working toward offering participants on this program and other interested parties the opportunity to undertake the PMP examination in Ireland in 1996.

ISRAEL

STATUS OF THE PROJECT MANAGEMENT PROFESSION

In general, at what stage is the project management profession in your country today (i.e., newly introduced, growing, mature)? Please comment.

Project management in Israel is very advanced and continuously growing. The growth is presented via quite a few project management programs, shorts and longs, that are offered by either academic institutes or companies. In the next academic year we are going to offer, in the School of Business Administration at Tel Aviv University, a 200-hour project management program tailored to managers. In our school we teach the basic project management course to around 250 students per year.

What industries or types of projects are the main users of modern project management in your country or region today?

Surprisingly enough, most of our students come from the high-tech industry, and very few come from the construction industry. However, there is a vast interest in companies that organize internal project management workshops.

What industries or areas of application in your country have the greatest need for more or better project management? What industries or organizations offer the greatest opportunities for growth of professional project management in your country? Why?

The types of projects that require better project management are either the very large and complex ones such as the construction of a power station, or high-tech projects that deal with relatively new concepts. It is important to comment that the public sector in general requires better project management even in simple projects.

How can the project management profession be most effectively advanced in your country?

Possible ways to advance project management in Israel are to:
- Have an active project management chapter
- Initiate project management certificates
- Develop advanced courses in project management.

What impact will globally recognized project management standards or certification have on the project management profession in your country?

A globally recognized project management standard will enhance the field because it will encourage companies to send their employees to formal training where they will be exposed to more advanced techniques.

ISSUES OF COMMON GLOBAL INTEREST

What should be contained in a global Project Management Body of Knowledge (PMBOK)?

In establishing the global PMBOK one should differentiate between methodological issues, which are not regionally dependent, and local issues. For example, scheduling is a methodological issue, whereas law is a local one. Some issues are both, such as contracts.

How important will international "Standards" for project management be in your country or region? Please comment.

See "What impact will globally recognized ..." and "What should be contained in a global ..." above.

Is project management certification of interest in your country? What type of project management certification?

As it stands right now, project management certification is of no interest in Israel. However, since we believe that it is an important issue, we will make a point to introduce it. We plan to have the first project management certificate exam in Israel in June 1996.

What is your interest or position on a unified global project management association or organization? If you support such an organization, how should it be organized and for what objectives?

We are in favor of having a global project management association since many projects require integrated efforts in a few countries at the same time. The board of directors of such an organization should consist of regional representatives.

How can project management associations around the world better communicate and cooperate to advance the project management profession?

As it stands right now there is no specific body of knowledge that should be treated separately concerning a global project. As the first step the institute should develop a list of relevant global issues to be addressed.

YOUR ORGANIZATION

Briefly describe the history, purpose, organization and activities of the professional project management organization you represent.

We belong to the Management of Technology area at the School of Business Administration in Tel Aviv University. Project management is a major subject within our area, that attracts many graduate students. Also, we offer quite a few workshops and seminars for executives.

Does your organization have established relations with agencies or departments of your government, or with universities? Please describe.

As it stands right now we do not have any formal contacts with the government, but we do have a lot of informal contact with professionals throughout the whole country.

ITALY

STATUS OF THE PROJECT MANAGEMENT PROFESSION

In general, at what stage is the project management profession in your country today (i.e., newly introduced, growing, mature)? Please comment.

Project management in Italy is growing, but not homogeneously. In some industry sectors it could be considered to be mature (e.g., engineering and construction, aerospace), in others it is in its infancy (e.g., banking and insurance, information technology, public services), and in yet others (e.g., telecommunications, civil construction) it is somewhere in between. (Recent legislation requiring that project management be used on all public works contracts should contribute to the diffusion of project management, but the guidelines given in this legislation are still sufficiently vague to allow political interference.)

There has been a general, gradual awareness creeping across the country over the last 10 years or so. Lots of people in all industries talk about it, but most do little, mainly because they do not have the power, the experience of "selling" it to their top management, or have sufficient real knowledge of the project. A good example of this is in manufacturing, where project management has had mixed success.

Awareness programs are carried out mainly by the Project Management Section of ANIMP (the National Association of Italian Engineering and Construction enterprises), which has an annual national seminar and holds half-day seminars aimed at the use of project management in a variety of industries. In addition, some of the vendors of software products for the sector have user association meetings that provide some general education and help to create awareness.

> I've been a "project management missionary" in Italy for 23 years now ... I can say that now, at least, people are talking about it, although it's still viewed as something that's used only in engineering/construction. We need training, education, and awareness programs—an international certification would help.
>
> David Mathie, ANIMP

What industries or types of projects are the main users of modern project management in your country or region today?

Difficult to answer this one. It depends on one's understanding (the definition) of modern project management. However, as said above, the main thrust of management in engineering and construction companies is to use modern project management methodologies, techniques and software support tools to "manage by projects," although most do not, at least officially, recognize their management as such.

The main types of projects in which project management is used are industrial engineering projects and large infrastructure projects; e.g., construction of Italy's high-speed rail system. (Project management is also used by the principal Italian makers of the rolling stock for high-speed rail systems.)

What industries or areas of application in your country have the greatest need for more or better project management? What industries or organizations offer the greatest opportunities for growth of professional project management in your country? Why?

Public services is probably the sector in greatest need of more and better project management, notwithstanding recent legislation that requires the use of project management in public service contracts. The driver of this legislation was the European Union requirement for Italy to align itself with EU regulations and legislation in relation to providing equal opportunities on public service contracts for enterprises throughout the EU. (There was much political resistance and the result is a fairly "toothless" law which, however, is a very welcome step in the right direction.)

The industrial sectors that will provide the most opportunity are manufacturing (medium-sized enterprises—most of Italy's industry is small to medium-sized) and financial services (banking and insurance). Information technology is another area of opportunity and the developments in this field are such that the rate of change is inducing (or should be) management to look for ways to leverage their investment in information technology. This is creating a groundswell of interest in project management as a management tool in the industry.

How can the project management profession be most effectively advanced in your country?

Through awareness and education programs carried out at national level by a truly "independent" organization that is acceptable across all industrial sectors. Notwithstanding the fact that there has been a project management association active in Italy for about 15 years (the Project Management Section of ANIMP), that has done a lot to increase the awareness of project management in Italy, there is still no recognized independent organization that can fulfill the role of "leader" in the promotion of project management across the spectrum of industries and agencies in the country.

The Project Management Section of ANIMP does a very good job but it has the limitation of being perceived as ANIMP; to become a member of the Project Management Section, one has to be also, or first, a member of ANIMP. Although there are a number of our members from telecommunications, manufacturing, and other industrial sectors, the great majority are from the engineering and construction sector. Many people and organizations who would be otherwise interested in joining are put off by this aspect. They believe— maybe wrongly—that the accent of the association is heavily biased towards engineering and construction and that, therefore, there is not enough for them to gain from being a member.

However, our continuing commitment to education is paying off—albeit quite slowly—and we are reaching many more people from outside engineering and construction today than we were a few years ago. A sample from our 1995 education program follows:
- General course for project managers
- General course for proposal managers
- Project risk management
- Project management in manufacturing

- Project management in civil construction
- Safety in project engineering and construction
- Evaluation of work progress during construction
- Critical phases of projects.
- Feasibility studies in private and public service companies.

What impact will globally recognized project management standards or certification have on the project management profession in your country?

Again a difficult one to answer. One of the big problems is achieving recognition by "government" of project management as a profession, a situation that is fairly common across European countries, and then agreeing on recognized standards for certification. Therefore, globally recognized standards would be very welcome, and would help in our negotiations with national educational bodies. Our organization is working within IPMA toward producing core European standards; we also have the intention of creating a certification program that reflects IPMA standards for Italy.

ISSUES OF COMMON GLOBAL INTEREST

What should be contained in a global Project Management Body of Knowledge (PMBOK)?

Our organization believes that the new structure of the PMBOK, covering 9 fundamental topics, is fine as the basis for the core knowledge required for project managers. However, perhaps topics covering the political and financial aspects of project management should be included.

As the various associations around the world solidify their own experience, documented as "Bodies of Knowledge," maybe this could be included in some form of "Global PMBOK" acceptable to both the profession and industry, which could provide the basis for certification and could serve as a basic international accreditation.

How important will international "Standards" for project management be in your country or region? Please comment.

Those organizations and enterprises that work in the "export" sector have to follow international standards in order to be competitive, so any recognized international standards are very important. Nationally, standards are important and the public service sector follows those defined by recent legislation. In general, Italian standards are becoming ever closer to European standards. Italian industry will have to focus on European and other international standards in the future.

Is project management certification of interest in your country? What type of project management certification?

It is of undeniable interest, but this interest has fluctuated over the years. It could be said that interest is growing again, mainly within the profession. It is difficult to judge the degree of interest in sectors outside of engineering and construction, where interest is mainly related to international requirements.

Our organization is very interested and, we will follow the IPMA lead in this area.

What is your interest or position on a unified global project management association or organization? If you support such an organization, how should it be organized and for what objectives?

We are very supportive. The idea of having global cooperation among associations has been on the table, especially IPMA and PMI, for a number of years. Advances have been made on all sides (via the various cooperation agreements between PMI and IPMA) and maybe this is the time that tangible agreement could be achieved toward something more substantial. It would be necessary to create a platform that satisfies the differences in culture and mentality of the various geographical regions. For example, it is our feeling that European culture and mentality are more oriented toward the methods and philosophy rather than to the tools. One objective could be to find a common language and a common approach to problems.

It is implicit that any global "federation" be based on the recognition of national and regional bodies; that qualification/certification be, in some way, interchangeable; and that national/regional cultural needs be fully represented.

A "global" association could be organized on a regional basis, with industry "groups" cutting through the regions; or vice versa. The mechanics of this would have to be worked out equitably in accordance to the "power" and representation of the existing bodies, and in relation to what they "bring to the table." We would want to avoid a United Nations type of situation where politics consume most of the energy. We would also need to overcome inter-society, or inter-association, rivalries such that representation of members from any "local" or "international" association (e.g., ANIMP, PMI or IPMA) would be through delegates from any one, or more than one, of these associations.

The questions: Do the professional associations have a real mandate from their members? Is there, or has there been, sufficient time to prepare a "vision" and, if so, has this been communicated to all sufficiently well? Do we need to do this? Are there any examples of global associations of recognized professionals (e.g., architects) from which we could learn and take guidance? Maybe the AICE/ICEC experience could help, and it could be that it is the closest to what we have in mind.

As project management professionals we should recognize that change for the better is a good thing. An opportunity, which has quite a short "window," exists to actually reach agreement to establish a global federation of project management associations, if we can overcome parochialisms and regional biases, etc. This would be a good thing. To achieve it, we have to insist that our "leaders" actually show true leadership and develop the "vision" for the future; they are the "change leaders." They have to develop strategies for producing the changes in the internal processes of the existing organizations that are necessary to achieve the vision. They have to define new directions and communicate these to those who understand the vision and are committed to its realization, and who can create the coalitions necessary to assist the process. A "movement" has already started. The leaders of the main associations involved have to maintain this movement, they have to maintain the direction and they have to ensure that the proper input is given to overcome obstacles to the changes that are necessary to achieve the vision. The window of opportunity is closing all the time; we have to reach agreement now if we want to ensure that the opportunity does not slip from our grasp.

The objectives of a global federation would be:
- Coordinating the development, and the maintenance, of agreed upon international standards for knowledge, competence, etc., for the profession of project management
- Providing a means of communication between national associations and for the co-ordination of activities at the international level
- Providing a means for responding to the requirements of national associations
- Providing a channel for the interaction and cross-fertilization of ideas and new developments in the profession
- Providing a forum for communication between project management professionals who have international interests.

How can project management associations around the world better communicate and cooperate to advance the project management profession?

To some extent the answer is given above in the objectives of a global federation. Networking between professionals in various parts of the world already takes place on a personal basis. Of course we also have to motivate and inspire the continuation and widening of this, and it could be improved if we had a structured forum at global level. We also have to create the interest.

Currently, the membership of multiple organizations allows people from different nations and associations an insight into what others are doing, via the publications of the various national organizations to which these professionals belong. However, this is somewhat cumbersome and some means should be explored as to how these professionals can get access to the content of these publications without necessarily being a member of the publishing organization. A global association could be part of the answer as the Internet is part of the answer today. Maybe we should set up a PM site on the "Net," if it has not already been done. This, however, is only helpful to those who are in a geographical region that has good communications; there are still many parts of the world where it is difficult to access Internet.

YOUR ORGANIZATION

Briefly describe the history, purpose, organization and activities of the professional project management organization you represent.

The association had its origins in the engineering and construction industry. A group of project managers got together about 15 years ago and started the first serious discussions on how to form an association. The leaders of this group were already international members of Internet (now IPMA) and the focus was on forming an Italian association that could be part of the Internet family.

The outcome was that the association was formed within ANIMP, mainly because the members of the group were nearly all from enterprises associated within ANIMP, but also the problem of initial financing was overcome in this way. ANIMP registered with Internet as the official Italian Project Management Association (it was the only one and still is) and we were on our way.

Milan-based, the association is a Section of ANIMP and is governed by an elected board of 11 members. Elections are held every two years; each dues-paid member of the Section has a single vote; and the chairman is chosen by the board from the elected board members.

The main objectives of the association are to:
- Promote a professional approach to, and to advance the discipline of, project management
- Provide a forum for project management across all industrial sectors, thereby increasing cross-fertilization of ideas and communication
- Increase awareness of project management at all levels within society.

The association is the only Italian organization that provides a forum for project management in the country. The association is a non-profit organization and is a voluntary body that works for the benefit of its members. It also attempts to provide a unifying influence for project management across all industrial sectors.

Our membership has fluctuated over the years and we have 149 dues-paid members today. Membership has decreased in recent years, reflecting the harsh economic climate and other difficulties that Italy has had to face during this period.

Service to our members includes a monthly journal *Impiantistica Italiana* (Italian Engineering) published by ANIMP and a quarterly newsletter, "Project Management News."

With the aim of increasing the strength of the association, our main strategies for the future are to:
- Continue our efforts to spread the presence of our association throughout the country
- Launch a project management certification program (in symbiosis with IPMA).

We are implementing this strategy by increasing our contacts with universities and, to increase our visibility and allow us to create local working groups and increase our appeal, by establishing a number of local reference points in other cities. We have just established a local reference point at the University La Sapienza in Rome.

Does your organization have established relations with agencies or departments of your government, or with universities?

We have close relations, via ANIMP, with other national industry associations (e.g., OICE – Organization of Italian Construction Engineering companies) and with academia. The Italian association is part of ANIMP, which has a number of university professors on its board, many of whom have an increasing interest in project management. We have no relations with government agencies because these have little or no interest in us and are not receptive, notwithstanding the recent legislation related to the use of project management in public works contracts.

JAPAN

STATUS OF THE PROJECT MANAGEMENT PROFESSION

In general, at what stage is the project management profession in your country today (i.e., newly introduced, growing, mature)? Please comment.

The stage of maturity of the project management profession in Japan can be classified as growing on an overall scale. There is wide variety of project management maturity, depending on the industry affiliation, as follows:
- Engineering and construction: Mature, with 40 years of project management practice
- General construction: Growing to mature
- Manufacturing: Newly introduced
- Information services industry: Newly introduced to growing
- Public services: Virtually not introduced yet.

What industries or types of projects are the main users of modern project management in your country or region today?

The engineering and construction companies operating in oil and gas, chemical, industrial, and large infrastructure projects are the main users of modern project management in Japan; all of these companies engineer and build plants worldwide.

> ENAA concluded a general cooperation agreement with PMI back in 1979 and since then we have maintained a very fruitful relationship with PMI, and now we look upon this forum as an exciting springboard to expand our cross-fertilization network, starting today.
>
> Hiroshi Tanaka, ENAA

What industries or areas of application in your country have the greatest need for more or better project management? What industries or organizations offer the greatest opportunities for growth of professional project management in your country? Why?

The general construction industry will draw on more comprehensive project management processes as the size and complexity of their construction projects grow and as needs for construction management are further identified. The manufacturing industries will start realizing the benefits of project management with an increasing share of project-style business operations.

How can the project management profession be most effectively advanced in your country?

The project management profession can be advanced through the strong initiatives of ENAA and its Project Management Committee as Japan's sole association that promotes project management; such initiatives include joint research on project management technology issues, seminars and workshops, cooperation with PMI and other professional associations on issues of common interest, and publicity activities on project management toward the Japanese industry.

The ongoing changes of the Japanese industrial circles for globalization and more professional services orientation will generally help advance the project management profession.

What impact will globally recognized project management standards or certification have on the project management profession in your country?

Globally recognized project management standards will be welcomed by project management professionals in Japan as they can reference their efforts for professional advancement primarily to such global standards as a baseline. If we look at industry, however, the degree of their impact will vary with the industry affiliation. Each industry branch is interested most in international standards or certification having specific impacts on the industry branch in question; as such there are branches of industry in which project management standards or certification may not exert a primary impact.

ISSUES OF COMMON GLOBAL INTEREST

What should be contained in a global Project Management Body of Knowledge (PMBOK)?

We consider that both the revised PMBOK of PMI and the Core Framework for Project Management Knowledge being prepared by a group of PMI-IPMA-APM-AIPM-ENAA representatives are well organized Project Management Body of Knowledge documents that deserve recognition as a global PMBOK.

The revised PMBOK to be released soon could be recognized, as it is, as global project management Body of Knowledge *as a full version.* It covers all the essential elements of project management that can selectively apply to projects of particular types and regardless of project locations, and the PMBOK admits such selective application.

The Core Framework for Project Management Knowledge, while still under preparation, will be a fine *short version* of PMBOK, which will provide a framework and will leave details to each country/region/industry.

How important will international "Standards" for project management be in your country or region? Please comment.

An international standard for project management is valuable since there is no local version.

Is project management certification of interest in your country? What type of project management certification?

The answer is mixed. There are always supporters of some types of project management certification as a target of professional advancement and as proof of professional proficiency; however, there is, as yet, no consensus on the type of project management certification.

It is, however, noted that the category of Project Engineering has recently been introduced into the Japanese system of state qualification of professional engineers. The Project Engineer defined here is more a Project Manager than an engineer, and there is a growing interest in this title among contractors' project managers and project engineers.

Regarding PMP certification, there is very limited Japanese interest in the original (English) PMP examination.

What is your interest or position on a unified global project management association or organization? If you support such an organization, how should it be organized and for what objectives?

Neither ENAA nor its Project Management Committee is in a position to be part of a unified project management association since ENAA is not a professional association but rather is an engineering services industry association of business firms. However, ENAA would be most pleased to maintain a cooperation agreement with such a unified project management association, once established, as it now does with PMI.

To be successful, such a unified organization should not cluster around countries or regions but should consist of streams of project management professionals along industry branches while operating functional committees across industry branches. Area- or city-based local chapters, as with PMI, would be a prerequisite for fostering fundamental professional advancement.

How can project management associations around the world better communicate and cooperate to advance the project management profession?

Associations should first agree on principal themes of joint pursuit for the advancement of the project management profession and on the way to follow up on them through regular contacts. The Global Project Management Forum will be an excellent opportunity to lay the foundation for enhanced communication and cooperation among project management associations.

YOUR ORGANIZATION

Briefly describe the history, purpose, organization and activities of the professional project management organization you represent.

ENAA was established in August 1978 as a non-profit organization dedicated to the promotion and capability enhancement of the Japanese engineering services industry. ENAA is participated in by Japanese engineering services and related companies and is supported by the Ministry of International Trade and Industry (MITI). ENAA's Project Management Committee is a division of its Project Engineering Committee (steering organ) and has existed since the foundation of ENAA.

The ENAA Project Management Committee has such broad objectives as:
- Advance the project management capability level of the overall industry through cross-fertilization.
- Conduct collective research on the state-of-the-art of project management.
- Provide, through combined efforts, practical solutions to project operations issues.
- Provide a forum for professional development in project management.

The committee is currently represented by 46 companies (engineering and construction companies and large manufacturing companies having contracting engineering divisions). Its activities are carried out through committee meetings, steering member meetings, research by funded research task forces and non-funded study groups, and seminars.

The current themes of emphasis in the committee include the globalization of Japanese companies, cross-industry approach to project management practices, and competitiveness

in project management technologies. Over the past three years, the committee has produced the following deliverables, among others:
- Cost Engineering in the '90s (1992)
- Contemporary Project Management Information Systems (1993)
- Broad CAE—Integration of CAE and PMS.

Does your organization have established relations with agencies or departments of your government, or with universities? Please describe.

ENAA is officially supported by the MITI as mentioned above. It has no established relationship with Japanese universities since they have no comprehensive project management curricula.

KOREA

STATUS OF THE PROJECT MANAGEMENT PROFESSION

In general, at what stage is the project management profession in your country today (i.e., newly introduced, growing, mature)? Please comment.

In general, the project management profession in Korea is considered to be at the newly introduced stage. However, there is growing concern for the project management profession in the construction industry and utility areas.

What industries or types of projects are the main users of modern project management in your country or region today?

The construction industry and utilities are the main users of modern project management.

What industries or areas of application in your country have the greatest need for more or better project management? What industries or organizations offer the greatest opportunities for growth of professional project management in your country? Why?

Construction, utilities and R&D areas have the greatest need for more or better project management. Especially the utility area offers the greatest opportunities for the growth of professional project management, considering the enormous amounts of money involved and its significant impact on other industries.

> As an indication of Korean interest in project management, 42 members of our organization are participating in this Seminar/Symposium. We are introducing the PMP system into our country, and will continue until a global PM certification is in place.
>
> Jong Shin Kim, PROMAT

How can the project management profession be most effectively advanced in your country?

We believe that PROMAT, a non-profit professional organization, has offered such services as annual symposia, seminars, educational classes and journals to the nationwide project management professionals and has to be fostered for the rapid advancement of the project management profession in Korea. At the same time, international technology exchange with professional organizations such as PMI and IPMA has to be increased.

What impact will globally recognized project management standards or certification have on the project management profession in your country?

Since project management is a newly introduced profession in Korea, global project management standards or certification might be a good guideline for the future direction of our project management profession, education and certification.

ISSUES OF COMMON GLOBAL INTEREST

What should be contained in a global Project Management Body of Knowledge (PMBOK)?
We think the contents of the current PMBOK is well inclusive.

How important will international "Standards" for project management be in your country or region? Please comment.
The necessity of international standards for project management might be increasing for the rapid information exchange in the globalized society.

Is project management certification of interest in your country? What type of project management certification?
It is a help for us to use as is until our system develops. If an international certification is introduced for global use, the adoption of the system will be positively considered in our country.

What is your interest or position on a unified global project management association or organization? If you support such an organization, how should it be organized and for what objectives?
Once there is consensus among project management associations, we think a unified global project management association can serve as an effective and authoritative role for the global project management profession.

The purpose of the organization may be to promote cooperation among national and multi-national project management associations worldwide for their mutual well-being and that of their individual members.

A member of the unified organization can be a national or multinational project management association or organization that is non-profit.

How can project management associations around the world better communicate and cooperate to advance the project management profession?
By establishing an advisory committee consisting of representatives from project management associations around the world and publishing a global project management directory by which various contacts could be naturally made between individuals.

YOUR ORGANIZATION

Briefly describe the history, purpose, organization and activities of the professional project management organization you represent.
PROMAT (Korean Institute of Project Management and Technology) is made up of 593 individual professionals, 106 students, and 54 corporate members. Although the large number of corporate members is in the engineering/ construction sector, software, consultants, manufacturing, research and development, utilities are also represented.

PROMAT was founded in 1991 as the only non-profit organization for project management in Korea.

The organization's goal is "to promote national project management technical capabilities and to foster international technology exchange in the area of project management."

Members participate in annual technical symposia, training courses, quarterly breakfast meetings and special presentations, and receive a quarterly magazine and other technical papers and publications.

PROMAT is a member society of ICEC (International Cost Engineering Council) and has also entered into a cooperation agreement with PMI of the United States.

Does your organization have established relations with agencies or departments of your government, or with universities? Please describe.

PROMAT has maintained close relations with government: Ministry of Science and Technology, Ministry of Trade Industry and Energy, Ministry of Construction and Transportation.

PROMAT has provided educational services in cooperation with universities and many professors are involved in our technical committee.

KUWAIT

STATUS OF THE PROJECT MANAGEMENT PROFESSION

In general, at what stage is the project management profession in your country today (i.e., newly introduced, growing, mature)? Please comment.

The project management profession is growing in Kuwait as compared to its neighbors. It was introduced in the early 1980s, and since then there is more awareness in Kuwait that project management is an option to manage projects.

What industries or types of projects are the main users of modern project management in your country or region today?

Large scale building construction projects and petrochemical/oil sector projects.

What industries or areas of application in your country have the greatest need for more or better project management? What industries or organizations offer the greatest opportunities for growth of professional project management in your country? Why?

- Non-building type construction projects (such as high ways, pipelines, etc.)
- Medium scale construction projects
- Utilities projects
- Environmental projects.

Industries or organizations that offer the greatest opportunities for growth of professional project management in Kuwait are the oil/refineries sector and the construction sector.

The reasons are: there is precedence or track records for these types of projects, in which one can witness the effect of project management on managing projects. Also, Kuwait is an oil state, and it is expected that the oil industry will last and improve for many decades to come.

• • • • • • • • • • • •

Our small country became famous after the Gulf crisis; Kuwait is half the size of New Jersey, but has 10 percent of the world's oil. So project management is expanding in the oil sector; this means that our government is the largest user of project management and the government must play a major role in expanding [the discipline] in Kuwait.

• • • • • • • • • • • •

Hashem Al-Tabtabi
Kuwait University

How can the project management profession be most effectively advanced in your country?

- By government embracing project management as a profession, since government is the largest user of modern project management.
- By continuing project management training to create awareness.
- By education in project management through universities and colleges.

What impact will globally recognized project management standards or certification have on the project management profession in your country?

There will be some impact on globally recognized project management standards or certification on the project management profession in Kuwait. However, Kuwait is so much attached to what is surrounding it. Therefore, it is suggested that these standards be adopted by countries like Saudi Arabia and Egypt so that it may carry the maximum impact on Kuwait.

ISSUES OF COMMON GLOBAL INTEREST

What should be contained in a global Project Management Body of Knowledge (PMBOK)?

The following should be contained in a global project management body of knowledge.
- Unified terminology or common language, for example multipackages and fast track vs. phased construction
- Political risk management
- International or multicultural aspects
- Technology transfer of project management to undeveloped countries.

How important will international "Standards" for project management be in your country or region? Please comment.

It will be important to have international standards for project management because:
- International firms bring in different methods and procedures to manage projects and these only last for the duration of the project.
- It will upgrade the understanding of project management as a profession to many who still do not know the concept of project management as a profession.

Is project management certification of interest in your country? What type of project management certification?

Currently project management certification is not known and recognized in Kuwait. However, it can be of interest if people know about it and its importance.

What is your interest or position on a unified global project management association or organization? If you support such an organization, how should it be organized and for what objectives?

It will be a good thing to spread the concept of project management through a unified global project management association. I do support such an organization and would like to discuss further procedures on the way to organize such an organization.

How can project management associations around the world better communicate and cooperate to advance the project management profession?

No comment.

YOUR ORGANIZATION

Briefly describe the history, purpose, organization and activities of the professional project management organization you represent.

I work full time with the Department of Civil Engineering, the College of Engineering and Petroleum, Kuwait University. The current activities are teaching project management courses, research and consultation in project management.

Does your organization have established relations with agencies or departments of your government, or with universities?

Our organization has a well established relationship with agencies of Kuwait government through its unit the "Office of Consultation and Career Development." This unit provides the Kuwait community with consultation services and offers different training programs.

MEXICO

STATUS OF PROJECT MANAGEMENT PROFESSION

In general, at what stage is the project management profession in your country today (i.e., newly introduced, growing, mature)? Please comment.

The profession is not recognized at this moment. The project manager in Mexico works by feeling (intuition), as there is not an institution or professional organization dedicated to impart knowledge on this matter.

When I received your invitation, I contacted several institutions in Mexico, and there is not an institution that handles this matter even at the lowest level.

What industries or types of projects are the main users of modern project management in your country or region today?

The main users of project management are users "by feeling." At this time the main users are related to construction, chemical industries, petrochemical, metallurgic, banking and consulting firms.

What industries or areas of application in your country have the greatest need for more or better project management? What industries or organizations offer the greatest opportunities for growth of professional project management in your country? Why?

In my opinion, they are the same industries as mentioned in the previous response. The construction industry offers the greatest opportunities in Mexico because in this industry, project management is the first step.

How can the project management profession be most effectively advanced in your country?

Professionalizing or creating specialists on the matter. Any organization should have a project management department in order to get better results.

What impact will globally recognized project management standards or certification have on the project management profession in your country?

I think the effect of this would produce great benefits in any organization because with this we would avoid improvisation and risk—things that have damaged Mexico a lot. We should work under specific standards and with experts.

> We have the same problem as Brazil with unfinished projects. [It] is not productivity or efficiency, but the need for skills. We are a demanding society, a society in political and economic transition …we have NAFTA challenges and opportunities before us as well as global challenges and opportunities. We welcome your support in our scheme of organizing our society through the management of projects.
>
> Oscar de Lasse,
> Calpan, S.A.

ISSUES OF COMMON GLOBAL INTEREST

What should be contained in a global Project Management Body of Knowledge (PMBOK)?

Information focused on each field and invitations to training courses all over the world.

How important will international "Standards" for project management be in your country or region? Please comment.

They will be very important because we are involved in a world of continuous changes and one can no longer work within a country and ignore the exterior. At this moment, with competitors from all over the world, companies that work on a local or regional basis are losing business. Moreover, with the NAFTA agreement, Mexico must compete and prepare to be better, and ready to beat any competitor or at least be equal to the best.

Is project management certification of interest in your country? What type of project management certification?

Not at this moment. Project management is not yet recognized in this country, but in the future, I'm sure one will need to be certified to work as a project manager.

I suggest that the minimum certification should be at least a certificate-diploma or implement this as a master's degree program.

In the future, I intend to get a certification from Project Management Institute because with this I am sure anyone can demonstrate the capability of working anywhere.

What is your interest or position on a unified global project management association or organization? If you support such an organization, how should it be organized and for what objectives?

I don't have any specific interest, but I would be glad to participate in any organization of project management based in Mexico since I am one of the few PMI members actually registered. In my opinion, it is necessary to unify standards so that work can be the same in all places. To organize it, there must be a representative of each country who continuously notifies the organization about the changes in the field of his or her country. Right now, things and technology change every day.

After this, the same organization could be an investor or stockholder of different projects in countries where development is needed. There is a need to take technology and knowledge to many underdeveloped places. It would be very interesting to create something like that because the Project Management Institute is a universe of knowledge and anyone can contribute to the countries already mentioned.

How can project management associations around the world better communicate and cooperate to advance the project management profession?

It is very easy to communicate all over the world through the Internet.

YOUR ORGANIZATION

Briefly describe the history, purpose, organization and activities of the professional project management organization you represent.

Even though I am registered under Construcciones Albyaca, at the moment I am the special project director of a company named Calpan, so I will describe this group.

Calpan Group emerged in 1971 as a builder. In 1974, Calpan began focusing on housing, because of the strong demand, and transformed into a housing promoter. In the beginning, Calpan worked for a few years building low-cost houses for governmental institutions.

After 1974, Calpan continued working for the government, but also began negotiating directly with people who needed a house. Thus, Calpan was responsible for getting the money from the banks, making direct agreements with clients, and installing offices in each area where they built houses. By doing so, the banks were saved a lot of grief and Calpan collected its money faster by making steps easier for clients.

Calpan has been the winner of "Temo Del Sol," a prestigious award given by banking institutions in the housing field. This award is given in recognition to the best projects of low-cost housing in quality and price. The houses that Calpan builds and promotes are a project of houses that can be enlarged under specifications and procedures previously established.

In 1993, Calpan expanded into the hotel industry and is responsible for finishing the Comino Real Hotel, a 210-room hotel in Tuxtula Gutierrez, Chiapas.

Before 1994, Calpan established an agreement with governmental and private institutions to promote and support the challenge of housing production. Now due to the problems that the country has, it is necessary to get a new model where contractors, financial institutions, suppliers and the government join efforts to produce very low cost houses for people with low salaries. Every company needs to lower operational costs and sacrifice part of the profit, and Calpan has taken this challenge. For this reason, Calpan has not been working at the capacity it used to and had to decrease its size.

Because of this, I am committed to make a change in structure and do everything I can to help, so I am turning in a special report which I hope to present at the global forum for discussion. Calpan is planning new strategies for agreements with any organization interested in promoting the business of housing. Moreover, we are working on smaller houses so it will be easier for people to get affordable credit faster.

Does your organization have established relations with agencies or departments of your government, or with universities?

We have several agreements with different organizations.
- University of Chiapas: We recruit students who are one year away from graduating and train them to work for us (human resources project).
- State Government: The main objective is to build houses throughout Mexico, so it is necessary to establish agreements with different institutions for support. Mexico needs at least 700,000 houses.
- Saving Institutions: We are looking for new mechanisms to get investments in housing. With the agreement, any worker can save money monthly and later borrow the money from the institution to buy a house.

NEW ZEALAND

STATUS OF THE PROJECT MANAGEMENT PROFESSION

In general, at what stage is the project management profession in your country today (i.e., newly introduced, growing, mature)? Please comment.

Project management is definitely growing within New Zealand as a profession. The construction industry has a history of major projects (hydroelectric dams, geothermal power stations, oil and gas refineries, etc.). These projects tended to require the importation of skills to New Zealand, resulting in a strong contingent of foreign-qualified project managers. With their historical background the construction/engineering project managers are less open to change and more critical of attempts to standardize project management.

The IT industry is wakening to the need for project management, and there has been a gradual industry recognition that project management is more than time and cost control. The project managers involved in the industry are recognizing, with greater speed and enthusiasm than their management, the need to increase skills and develop greater depth, and carry a general excitement within our organization.

Commercial project management conferences, seminars and courses are becoming more readily available. The New Zealand Qualifications Authority is working through a set of guidelines for under- and postgraduate project management courses.

New Zealand can be described as a nation wishing project management to happen, but not yet possessing a clear direction.

> In our country of 3.2 million people and 60 million sheep, we have used project management mainly in coal mining and construction—and we also attribute our success in yacht racing [to project management]! Yet we often speak in New Zealand of the "maverick or cowboy project manager," the guy who acquires MS Project from the shop down the road and says, "I'm a project manager." There's a strong need for standards and for business to understand what project management is all about.
>
> Stephen Harrison, PMI-NZ

What industries or types of projects are the main users of modern project management in your country or region today?

Main industry users of project management include:

- Engineering/construction
- Information technology/communications
- Government works/road construction
- Energy.

What industries or areas of application in your country have the greatest need for more or better project management? What industries or organizations offer the greatest opportunities for growth of professional project management in your country? Why?

Information technology is the industry most in need of project management, and the most open to it. However, it is fair to say that all the industries would benefit because there is a diversity of knowledge, skills and expectations among all groups.

Organizations that are best placed to develop project management within New Zealand are:
- PMINZC—the only independent project management organization in the country
- Universities/Technical Institutes—a number of them are offering undergraduate and postgraduate courses, generally based on overseas courses (English or Australian)
- NZQA—Government qualifications authority responsible for establishing skills and knowledge standards, currently trying to do some catch-up on the industry.

How can the project management profession be most effectively advanced in your country?

By establishment of a recognized and neutral institution that establishes and publishes standards for project management method and practice. By introduction of a formal certification process that is regarded as worthy by industry in a similar light to professional certifications in law, accountancy, etc. These have started with the establishment of PMINZC.

What impact will globally recognized project management standards or certification have on the project management profession in your country?

Global standards would provide the stake in the ground to focus on. Currently the PMI PMBOK is accepted by our organization and is therefore the "accepted standard." However, with European, English and Australian influences featuring strongly in New Zealand project management there is a need to demonstrate international flavor, and this is seen as limited in the PMI PMBOK, which has a U.S. flavor.

ISSUES OF COMMON GLOBAL INTEREST

What should be contained in a global Project Management Body of Knowledge (PMBOK)?

PMI's PMBOK is a good start for a generalized body of knowledge. It would be beneficial to also include a technical section that covers:
- **Industry-based practices:** Outline specialist project management methods and practices by industry. This would raise general awareness of specific industry issues and practices to all project managers and enable cross-fertilization of ideas.
- **Geography-based practices:** If practices are utilized more strongly in a particular continent, nation or region, then the area should be identified. Examples include procurement methods with U.S. government acquisitions, which are of little direct relevance outside the United States but still add value through broadening global understanding of issues faced and approaches used.

- **International glossary:** Terms and meanings as they are used around the world, with annotation identifying region where term is used when it is restricted in its geographical use. This would assist professionals as the swing toward globally mobile project managers becomes more pronounced.

How important will international "Standards" for project management be in your country or region? Please comment.

Any standards would be important in New Zealand, and this is being focused on. Ideally, the standards should be as international as possible to:

- Increase general acceptance of the standard
- Cater to the international mix in the profession within New Zealand
- Assure greater depth and applicability of the knowledge base that forms the standard
- Provide a "common language" that facilitates easier interchange of ideas.

Is project management certification of interest in your country? What type of project management certification?

It is of moderate but growing interest. The PMI Project Management Professional (PMP) certification is the only program offered, and is seen as adequate by our organization. The same approach, with increased international flavor, would be a positive enhancement.

Another possible enhancement would be to introduce grades, with the current PMP (or equivalent) as the introductory grade. Higher grades would be based on increased depth and industry-specific knowledge. It is recognized that this would be a tall order to meet effectively, and may best be left to the universities and technical institutions, with input from project management organizations.

Increased emphasis on competency-based certification would be beneficial.

What is your interest or position on a unified global project management association or organization? If you support such an organization, how should it be organized and for what objectives?

It is strongly supported by the New Zealand PMINZC executive. The suggested organizational structure is:

- The decision making Executive should consist of a quorum of, say, 12 members.
- No more than one member from any project management organization (with the same organization in different countries being treated separately) should be on the Executive.
- The 3 to 5 largest international project management bodies should have permanent seats, with the remainder being provided by other organizations on a rotational basis.
- There should be a mechanism to assure that regional diversity and representation is maintained on the Executive.
- All project management organizations in a region would make submissions through their "regional" representative, irrespective of the organization from which he or she is from.

Objectives that the organization represents should include:
- Be the international professional and technical association in the field of project and program management, accepted and supported by the diverse organizations throughout the world.
- Achieve recognition through development and dissemination of the theory and practice of effective management of resources in reaching project goals.

How can project management associations around the world better communicate and cooperate to advance the project management profession?
- Advertise conferences of other organizations.
- Provide project management conferences that are developed across multiple project management bodies.
- Interchange articles/news, etc., between various publications.
- Establish a "What's Happening …" column in publications that identifies developments made in other project management organizations, and in terms of relationship building and joint ventures.
- Develop an electronic linkage between project managers and project management organizations.

YOUR ORGANIZATION

Briefly describe the history, purpose, organization and activities of the professional project management organization you represent.

Formation activities for the Project Management Institute New Zealand Chapter (PMINZC) commenced mid-1993. We are a chapter of the Project Management Institute and in March 1994 PMI formally issued our charter. Since then our membership has grown from 29 to 100. We expect this to dramatically increase over the next few months, as we are offering our first annual conference and this is gaining a great deal of national interest among various industries.

Our executive consists of 7 elected, voluntary members who manage their portfolios with the assistance of committees drawn from the membership. Portfolios cover membership, programs, professional development, and public relations.

Our mission is to promote awareness of PMINZC, develop project management knowledge and skills, foster communications and fellowship between PMINZC members and external organizations having a stake in project management professionalism.

Major activities include:
- Monthly newsletter, *PM Forum*, sent to all membership and potential members
- Membership lists circulated to membership quarterly (to enable networking)
- Monthly chapter meetings in Auckland Wellington, our two main centers
- Establishment of annual project management conference
- Preparation workshops (once a week for 16 weeks in Auckland and Wellington) prior to each PMP exam
- Offering the PMI PMP exam.

Does your organization have established relations with agencies or departments of your government, or with universities? Please describe.

We are currently establishing relationships with a number of universities and technical institutions. A number of our members are from these institutions and our ability to identify and influence project management course content is increasing. In general, we are still at the early stages, but the network is growing quickly. We have just agreed to assist one research study in project management practice being conducted by a technical institute, and hope to continue building on this into the future.

Work has started with the New Zealand Qualifications Authority in an effort to influence the skills and knowledge requirements in undergraduate and postgraduate courses offered throughout New Zealand.

NORWAY

STATUS OF THE PROJECT MANAGEMENT PROFESSION

In general, at what stage is the project management profession in your country today (i.e., newly introduced, growing, mature)? Please comment.

Norway has a long history of project management, beginning in the late 1950s, when construction of big hydropower plants came to an extensive stage, with Norway being the biggest hydropower producer in Europe. Norway being a small country of four million inhabitants, these big capital projects quickly developed an environment featuring a high standard of reliability in construction management/project management.

In the early 1970s, a great deal of oil and gas exploration took place offshore of Norway. During the past 25 years of extensive construction activities, Norway has reached the status of the second largest world exporter of oil and gas, with an investment rate of $6 billion–$8 billion (U.S.) per year. As offshore exploration has required bigger platforms in deeper and deeper water, complexity has increased as well as the pressure to be on schedule and on budget.

Based on this background, the relatively small project management environment in Norway has been developing for a half-century, under constant pressure to improve speed, as time is money in the oil industry. The economy has been good in the project management environment, with capability to research and develop new areas.

The project management environment reached prestige status when the Lillehammer Olympic Games were prepared. Most of the Lillehammer staff was recruited from the offshore oil industry—and they managed to be on time and within budget, with better quality than planned—as you have seen on television.

What industries or types of projects are the main users of modern project management in your country or region today?

Engineering companies related to the oil industry and the construction industry have been the main project management users until recently. Through projects, the main governmental bodies are making changes, especially the air control authorities, railways administration, road administration.

> There are 650 members in our Norwegian organization, a very good ratio in such a small country ... we have used project management for 25 years in the hydropower and offshore oil industries. When you reach the level that project management is at in Norway, you have to recharge the batteries. That is the value of getting together to hear new ideas, and that's why we like to have international conferences. [For example], I am interested in using this great profession in healthcare and hospitals. My company is developing a solution that looks at each patient as a project.
>
> Thor Gudmundsson
> NPMA, IPMA

What industries or areas of application in your country have the greatest need for more or better project management? What industries or organizations offer the greatest opportunities for growth of professional project management in your country? Why?

Opportunities for extending the project management borders exist in the public sector and in the service industries where there is a demand to improve management methods to systematic ways similar to those in the production industry. Since the price of oil has dropped, project management personnel have been moving into new industries and the public sector.

In addition, more and more project managers in the field of oil and gas exploration are now competing in the Middle East and Far East. The existing project management environment is extending the market for project management.

How can the project management profession be most effectively advanced in your country?

In order to build up a professional stand in project management, there is a demand to improve existing practice by attracting the best international project management trainers to international events in Norway. The Norwegian project management environment has organized several international events, such as ICEC '88, Nordnet '91, Internet '94 and International Expert Seminar '96.

The Norwegian environment has further been active in getting international recognition through accredited certification of project managers as well as by building up postgraduate education services in project management, i.e. master's and Ph.D. degrees.

What impact will globally recognized project management standards or certification have on the project management profession in your country?

In the multicultural, complex oil projects in Norway, with huge economic impact, there is a big risk due to lack of international standards and security of international recognized qualifications in project management. The impact of a common international standard would be to reduce risks, and to reduce the cost of control.

Norway has, in this aspect, played a leading role in establishing the European Centre for Complex Project and Contract Management (EPCI) in Stavanger for research in project management.

Extensive and remarkable results have been gained in shortening the timespan and reducing cost through the newly introduced NORSOK program, in which oil operators together with contractors have developed a new set of standards. Hopefully, this will lead to similar international co-operation.

ISSUES OF COMMON GLOBAL INTEREST

What should be contained in a global Project Management Body of Knowledge (PMBOK)?

Recognition of multicultural barriers to understanding has to be accepted, as a beginning. The terminology is imported, as a example, and there have been several misinterpretation of the words "qualification" and "certification" recently in IPMA.

How important will international "Standards" for project management be in your country or region? Please comment.

Being a small country, the demand for internationally recognized standards high, specially in the high-risk, capital-intensive oil industry with a multicultural short-term projects/processes.

Is project management certification of interest in your country? What type of project management certification?

For the professional project manager there is a demand for a proof of capability by becoming internationally recognized as a project manager. On the other hand, for the relatively highly educated/academic standards, the Norwegian project management professionals have no tradition of certifying skills, and the pressure to be certified is not there.

What is your interest or position on a unified global project management association or organization? If you support such an organization, how should it be organized and for what objectives?

For a small nation like Norway, global organization for professionalism in project management is a guarantee of internationally recognized qualifications as a project manager.

How can project management associations around the world better communicate and cooperate to advance the project management profession?

There is a demand for a communication channel, therefore let us start with one small step by establishing a common e-mail/web on the Internet.

YOUR ORGANIZATION

Briefly describe the history, purpose, organization and activities of the professional project management organization you represent.

No Response

Does your organization have established relations with agencies or departments of your government, or with universities?

No Response

The Global Status of the Project Management Profession

PAKISTAN

STATUS OF THE PROJECT MANAGEMENT PROFESSION

In general, at what stage is the project management profession in your country today (i.e., newly introduced, growing, mature)? Please comment.

Project management as a discipline is not new in Pakistan. In fact, it has its roots as far back as in the 1960s, when the Indus Basin Projects were undertaken and completed. Since then the profession has grown but is not properly organized. Today the importance of project management has been recognized, and more clients, consultants and contractors seek to employ either "project management" companies or individuals for implementation of their projects.

• • • • • • • • • • • •

Project management is not new in Pakistan (in fact, recently we were project managers for the World Cup in cricket), but more and more we are moving toward formalizing the project management system. I foresee that project managers will be able to fill a big gap, and to that end, I look forward to the establishment of a PMI Chapter in Pakistan.

• • • • • • • • • • • •

Rehan ul Ambia Riaz, PMI

What industries or types of projects are the main users of modern project management in your country or region today?

The principal users are the clients, sponsors and investors of large public projects. The users include the public sector and multinational companies. A few consulting engineering companies, management consultants and construction companies who are working on World Bank, ADB and IMF funded projects use project management techniques.

What industries or areas of application in your country have the greatest need for more or better project management? What industries or organizations offer the greatest opportunities for growth of professional project management in your country? Why?

The number one contender is the "large engineering projects sector," which encompasses Hyrdo power, highway construction, power projects and rural development projects (in water, health, education and social sectors) mostly funded by foreign agencies.

The industrial sector, which is now in the process of privatization, is second in line. Real estate development (including commercial, residential and recreational buildings and sports facilities) projects need to be implemented on project management principles because the sponsors now have developed great appreciation for the benefits rendered by the project management techniques.

How can the project management profession be most effectively advanced in your country?

There are a few professional institutions that provide classroom training on some aspects of project management but not a single academic institution or university has an organized project management curriculum. There have been numerous seminars on project management and construction management disciplines but they soon lose their effectiveness because there is no follow-up. In my opinion, the PMI chapter would be the best platform to launch a nationwide awareness for project management and then organize PMP examinations in Pakistan. Subsequently, academic institutions will be advised (through a PMI chapter) to introduce regular curricula on project management.

To further advance the application of project management, the Pakistan Engineering Council (a government regulatory body) will finally be approached to officially recognize the PMP as a prerequisite to practice project management.

What impact will globally recognized project management standards or certification have on the project management profession in your country?

As discussed earlier, there is a need for such internationally recognized project management standards or certification. However, some disciplines like legal and contractual conditions may have to be tailor-made according to local environments. Similarly, project management software may not be 100 percent applicable to local conditions.

ISSUES OF COMMON GLOBAL INTEREST

What should be contained in a global Project Management Body of Knowledge (PMBOK)?

Some of the things it should contain are:
- Standardization of basic project management principles
- Project categorization by nature, size and cost to determine applicability of project management techniques
- Listing of "project management systems" successfully applied to complete projects (categorized by size and nature)
- Directory of new systems being evolved and researched.

How important will international "Standards" for project management be in your country or region? Please comment.

Standards will require time and effort to develop a level of understanding and acceptability. First priority for our country is the establishment and recognition of the project management discipline.

Is project management certification of interest in your country? What type of project management certification?

Yes, of great interest.
All levels of project management certification will be welcomed.

What is your interest or position on a unified global project management association or organization? If you support such an organization, how should it be organized and for what objectives?

The most important step is to have PMI USA known at national level. If a PMI chapter is established in Pakistan, it would like to be associated on global basis. The principal object would be to share project management experience practically and have exchange of information on reciprocal basis.

How can project management associations around the world better communicate and cooperate to advance the project management profession?

In my opinion, the best way is to form associations and joint ventures amongst professional project management companies and implement projects at the international level. There could be an exchange of project management professionals between cooperating countries.

YOUR ORGANIZATION

Briefly describe the history, purpose, organization and activities of the professional project management organization you represent.

FTC Management Company (Pvt.) Limited was constituted in 1990 under Companies Ordinance 1984 by the following public sector organizations to carry out management, operation and maintenance and to take up similar assignments elsewhere and the project management of prestigious projects.

- National Development Finance Corporation
- Bankers Equity Limited
- House Building Finance Corporation
- Pak-Libya Holding Company (Pvt.) Limited
- Pak-Kuwait Investment Company (Pvt.) Limited
- Pakistan Automobiles Corporation
- Rice Export Corporation of Pakistan
- Cotton Export Corporation of Pakistan
- Trading Corporation of Pakistan
- Pakistan Steel Mills
- Canteen Stores Department.

Since its inception the company has undertaken major works, including the setting up of a team of highly qualified and experienced engineers in the field of management of operation and maintenance of buildings and project management.

At present we are undertaking the following jobs/projects:

- Project management of Arabian Sea Country Club, Bin Qasim, Karachi
- Project management of balance works of Shaukat Khanum Memorial Cancer Hospital and Research Centre, Lahore
- Project management of upgrade, renovation, additions and alterations of National Stadium, Karachi.
- Management, operation and maintenance of Finance and Trade Centre, Karachi (covered area 782,000 sq. ft. including power co-generation system with 2.8 MW capacity)
- Management, operation and maintenance of building services/systems of Civic Centre/Awami Markaz, Karachi (covered area approximately 145,000 sq. ft.)
- Management, operation and maintenance of building services/systems of ZAB Centre, Islamabad (covered area approximately 105,000 sq. ft.)
- Management, operation and maintenance of Gaddafi Stadium, Lahore.

Our company has to its credit a unique experience of managing almost all the phases of building complexes from initial planning to post-completion operation and maintenance.

Does your organization have established relations with agencies or departments of your government, or with universities? Please describe.

Yes.

Our company is owned by 11 large government-owned corporations as previously stated.

Similarly, our best clients are from the public sector.

Although we have no formal links with the universities, assistance is provided to the university students in conducting research and thesis work in the field of project and construction management.

RUSSIA

STATUS OF THE PROJECT MANAGEMENT PROFESSION

In general, at what stage is the project management profession in your country today (i.e., newly introduced, growing, mature)? Please comment.

Since the '30s, development and use of project management methods in Russia have been in line with world project management, but with a lag due to insufficient computerization and absent information technologies. In addition, a significant reason for this situation is a lack of a professional project management organization in the former USSR planned and distributive economy.

The beginning of intensive growth and application of modern project management relates to the end of 1990, when SOVNET—the Russian Association of Project Management—was created. The Association quite quickly entered the world community of project management professionals.

Today we can say that project management in Russia has a considerably developed theoretical and methodological base. At the same time, in the field of practical use, the project management profession in Russia could be characterized as "growing," because there is no significant experience with full project completion utilizing complex, modern project management methods.

> I will not speak about Russia—for that, you may read my report—but I would like to speak about this Global Forum ... the best thing for project management in developing and transitional economies would be the globalization and unification of project management, bringing world experience to all countries.
>
> Vladimir Voropajev,
> SOVNET, IPMA

What industries or types of projects are the main users of modern project management in your country or region today?

Nowadays in Russia the main spheres of modern project management application are:

- Gas, oil and fuel and energy industries
- New construction and reconstruction of housing, civil and industrial buildings and constructions, with a priority on housing
- Information and control systems
- Infrastructure with existing telecommunication and transport systems
- Metallurgy and mining industry
- Aerospace systems
- Agro-industrial complexes and logistics
- Conversion projects.

The main types of projects are:
- Technical
- Investment
- Innovation
- Organization.

What industries or areas of application in your country have the greatest need for more or better project management? What industries or organizations offer the greatest opportunities for growth of professional project management in your country? Why?

Due to reforms in Russia, modern project management methods are needed in programs and projects implemented in different branches of industry and production. These projects are connected with the social and economic conversion, as well as with technical upgrading and new technologies.

The greatest possibilities for project management development in Russian today are in the industrial sectors with favorable economic conditions. These opportunities include:
- Fuel and energy facilities
- Fossil fuel industries
- Industries that are related to food production and distribution
- Investment and financial credit spheres.

How can the project management profession be most effectively advanced in your country?

In the country today the effective promotion of project management is facilitated by the transition to the market economy, which dismantled the former planned and distributive system. The new economic situation demands a more thorough planning, preparation and implementation of projects with fixed budget and schedule, and for successful evaluation of project results. All this requires full scope project management implementation on a wide scale.

To be recognized as a necessity, the methodology of project management should be implemented in Russia. The following is required:
- Methods and means of project management should be created that meet specific features of the transition economy and peculiarities of the country
- Personnel training and qualification
- Wide support and popularization of project management in the mass media
- Legal support
- Encouragement and support of new project management professional organizations and institutions.

What impact will globally recognized project management standards or certification have on the project management profession in your country?

There are two distinct developments in Russia now. First, more and more Russian firms and organizations are joining world economic activity. Second, more and more foreign investors are participating in Russian projects and programs. Both of these processes require the creation of a united language of business communication and culture. In our opinion, modern project management with acknowledged standards of certification and accreditation can be a cultural bridge and provide a means of global business communication.

ISSUES OF COMMON GLOBAL INTEREST

What should be contained in a global Project Management Body of Knowledge (PMBOK)

The global project management Body of Knowledge should contain unified elements and a fundamental background developed with an international consensus. By essence, it should be an acknowledged basis of PMBOK developed in accordance with special features of economies, cultures and traditions of different countries of the world.

In this connection a global PMBOK should include:
- A worldwide understanding of the project management profession and ethics
- An integrated system of unified terms and definitions and a glossary
- A unified structure of PMBOK, with basic core and developing sections
- The contents of the unified PMBOK core
- A unified approach to the education and training of project management specialists, with differentiation on levels and degrees
- A basic program of personnel and education and training
- Unified requirements, program and procedures for certification of international project managers and specialized project management organizations
- Recommendations for national certification programs
- International standards and methodology recommendations on project management practical application involving invariant and variable components depending on the project's type, fields of use, type of country economy, etc.

How important will international "Standards" for project management be in your country or region? Please comment.

A global PMBOK, along with international project management standards, is of great importance for Russia because it will enable:
- A rapid overcoming of the gap in the development of professionalism and practical application
- An easy integration of Russia into the world economy and the enhancement of efficiency of Russian participation in foreign programs and projects
- An easy integration of the foreign firms and companies into the Russian economy and the other countries of the former USSR and efficient implementation of joint projects.

Is project management certification of interest in your country? What type of project management certification?

Undoubtedly, a certification in project management is of interest for Russia. The certification could include:
- Certification of Russian international project managers under a unified certification program
- Certification of Russian domestic project managers under unified program taking into account the national requirements.

What is your interest or position on a unified global project management association or organization? If you support such an organization, how should it be organized and for what objectives?

We think that global unification of the project management association and organizations is useful, necessary and timely. Our opinion is that such a unification could be done as a Federation of Project Management Associations (FPMA). An FPMA should not have a vertical hierarchy with bureaucratic apparatus but must be headed by a coordinated body that is elected by FPMA members, Elected representation should be for a period of 2–3 years.

The major FPMA objectives are:
- Global development of professionalism in project management and support of its promotion to new countries, regions and new fields of application
- Arrangement of FPMA members' cooperation in the professional field
- Support of global FPMA network development and involvement of new participants
- Representation of FPMA members in international organizations in the field of project management unification, international standards, education and certification
- Organizing and holding of world forums on project management
- Coordination of FPMA members' activity, assistance in FPMA members' liaison and communication
- Information servicing of FPMA members and publicity in project management.

How can project management associations around the world better communicate and cooperate to advance the project management profession?

The global promotion of the project management profession should be carried out by associations and organizations under the aegis of FPMA.

Actual problems and tasks of the organization should be resolved in the framework of special programs and projects of FPMA by executive teams of its member experts.

Financing of these projects and programs must be received from international financial and credit institutions and national organizations upon FPMA application.

YOUR ORGANIZATION

Briefly describe the history, purpose, organization and activities of the professional project management organization you represent.

The Russian Association of Project Management (Soviet Association before) was created on October 25, 1990, as a good-will union of project management professionals, and is a public non-profitable professional international organization acting under the Russian legislation and in accordance with the Statute of Association.

The highest body of the Association is the Conference which elects the board of the Association, the president, vice-presidents, CEO and the Executive Committee.

As of May 23, 1995, 53 organizations and 94 persons (among them experts from the United States, Egypt, Canada, Ukraine, Byelorussia, Estonia, Lithuania, Tadjikistan and

Kazakhstan) are members of SOVNET. The membership in SOVNET is of the following types:
- Corporate—for legal entities
- Collective—for republican, territorial, industrial associations or societies of project management
- Individual—for specialists in Project Management.

Those experts who have outstanding achievements in project management and/or have done great service to the Association are awarded the degree of the Honorary Member, with fixed benefits.

The main tasks of the Association are:
- Enhancement of project management state-of-the-art
- Forming of a professional project management market in Russia
- Rendering assistance to firms and organizations in defining the most suitable project management methods and means, as well as support in implementation of the methods
- Creation of a system of project management professional training (education, refresher training and certification).

For these SOVNET uses the following:
- **Informative and publishing activity.** SOVNET is gaining, analyzing, considering and promoting professional project management information and literature, as well as special publications of the Association.
- **Scientific activity**. This means searching for prospective trends, coordination and concentration of research and development of project management means and methods, arrangement of symposiums, conferences, meetings, exhibitions, etc. The Association has also created a unique library of domestic and foreign project management software.
- **Personnel training**. For this the Association develops scientific, methodological, educational and certification materials, participates in educational programs for students, refresher courses for experts and program certification.
- **Involvement in real industrial and social projects.** SOVNET has successfully developed concepts of creation and improvement of project management systems for civil construction in the country, in Moscow and in St. Petersburg, for Magnitogorsk metallurgical combine, etc.

Does your organization have established relations with agencies or departments of your government, or with universities? Please describe.

SOVNET actively participates in big industrial and social projects. Which means that the Association has maintained good relations with the following departments and organizations:
- The Government of Moscow—Departments of Development, Industry and Construction
- The Government of St. Petersburg
- The Ministry of Civil Construction of Russia

- The Ministry of Education
- The State Committee for Black Metallurgy
- The Ministry of Fuel and Energy
- The Ministry of Foreign Economic Relations—Tyazhpromexport
- RAO GASPROM
- The State Moscow Construction University
- The State St. Petersburg Architecture and Construction University
- The State Polytechnic University of Ekaterinburg
- The State Polytechnic University of Chelyabinsk
- The State Academy of Management.

All these organizations are members of the Association and customers of SOVNET consulting services.

The Global Status of the Project Management Profession

SAUDI ARABIA

STATUS OF THE PROJECT MANAGEMENT PROFESSION

In general, at what stage is the project management profession in your country today (i.e., newly introduced, growing, mature)? Please comment.

The project management profession has been developed extensively in the Gulf region. Over the past 50 years, the region has experienced incredible growth in the infrastructure and process industries arena.

What industries or types of projects are the main users of modern project management in your country or region today?

Both the process petroleum and infrastructure industries are the main users of project management in Saudi Arabia.

• • • • • • • • • • • •

[Our] 140 members are working diligently to develop the profession in the Gulf area. We have a great desire and intention to adopt an international approach to engineering standards and project management. PMI has great experience and knowledge: we should build on it, increase it.

• • • • • • • • • • • •

Khalid Alagil
PMI-Arabian Gulf Chapter

What industries or areas of application in your country have the greatest need for more or better project management? What industries or organizations offer the greatest opportunities for growth of professional project management in your country? Why?

I would guess that the mining industry will require the greatest need for project management since it is beginning to develop in the area. The greatest opportunities are still, however, in the petroleum and chemical industries. Petroleum and chemical related work remain the main revenue generating industries here in the Gulf and continue to attract the greatest interest in capital programs requiring project management.

How can the project management profession be most effectively advanced in your country?

Project management professionals can be developed and advanced through university-level programs dedicated to the skills required for project management. In the United States several technical universities have initiated programs in construction management and programmatic studies such as operations research and other programming skill type curriculums.

Architects are educated to manage entire building projects far more effectively than engineering students. Some of the techniques used for architects should be applied to the education of project management professionals.

What impact will globally recognized project management standards or certification have on the project management profession in your country?

It would help to dispel the myth that persons with high energy levels and limited experience and knowledge can manage projects effectively. It would also provide a minimum set of qualifications and skills for selection of working project managers.

ISSUES OF COMMON GLOBAL INTEREST

What should be contained in a global Project Management Body of Knowledge (PMBOK)?

The Body of Knowledge could use a section on cultural approaches and contracting strategies that are used throughout the world. As an example, in the Kingdom, the American approach to contracting with a client is a generally accepted practice. In the U.A.E, Bahrain and other Gulf countries, the British approach of using a key consultant is often used. Each approach puts the burden of liability on different parties.

How important will international "Standards" for project management be in your country or region? Please comment.

Over a period of time, they may be recognized. It depends on the enlightenment of the region leaders in the capital project industry.

Is project management certification of interest in your country? What type of project management certification?

Yes, we are getting more inquiries from our PMI Chapter members as to when and where the next project management Certification Exam will be.

What is your interest or position on a unified global project management association or organization? If you support such an organization, how should it be organized and for what objectives?

PMI-AGC is supporting this idea, but it is a long way off. First, the need for a project management association must be established, like the Boiler Code—out of need. Until it is apparent that there is a need, the ideas will be hard to push forward.

How can project management associations around the world better communicate and cooperate to advance the project management profession?

People in our business are always interested in case histories of projects to compare contracting philosophies, etc. It would be tremendous if PMI members could document projects, good and bad, for archiving. These case studies would be a source of discussion among the members and other associates as well as help prevent reoccurring problems.

> Last year, we had a conference in Bahrain, with 18 nations attending from the Far East, Europe and the States. This gives you an indication that the Arabian Gulf Chapter, though Arabian, encompasses many other countries.... People are demanding higher efficiency, higher quality, TQM, reengineering—both the buyers and the sellers...[and] changes in government structure and practices such as partnering and privatization also lead to an increased role for project management.
>
> Bassam Al-Tamini
> PMI-Arabian Gulf Chapter

The Global Status of the Project Management Profession

YOUR ORGANIZATION

Briefly describe the history, purpose, organization and activities of the professional project management organization you represent.

HISTORY

After an initial survey of interest of PMI members in Saudi Arabia and the Arabian Gulf Region in late 1991, Richard Hauptmann filed on April 10, 1992 a letter of intent, to form the Arabian Gulf Chapter.

An initial explanatory discussion was held in Al-Khobar on April 23, 1992, among Richard Johnson, Cliff Newcomb and Richard Hauptmann to plan formation of the chapter. Following this meeting, a membership campaign was launched featuring both individual contact and mailings.

As a result of this, on August 27, 1992, 16 people met for dinner at the Meridian Hotel in Al-Khobar, Kingdom of Saudi Arabia, to discuss the formation of a Project Management Institute Chapter in the Arabian Gulf area. It was agreed to proceed with formation of a chapter and interim officers were elected:

Richard C. Hauptmann, President
Saleh A. Al-Yami, Vice President
Edward H. Heard, Treasurer
Mohammed Abdulrahim, Secretary
Mike Roberts, Director of Membership

High interest in a Gulf Chapter was and continues to be apparent and with the second meeting in October of 1992, the membership committee was demonstrating results in increased registrations and attendance at the meetings. Thirty-six professionals attended this meeting. Our first speaker, Mr. W.A. Wenger, vice president and program manager of John Brown, Inc., spoke of their organization and approach to project management. As an indication of corporate support for the prospective chapter, Saudi Aramco sponsored this meeting.

The third meeting in December featured Mr. George Hull of Bechtel, Inc., who first came to Saudi Arabia in the late 1940s. He spoke on the development and construction of Jubail, a planned industrial city that was recently listed in *The Guinness Book of World Records* as the largest public works project ever built.

By December of 1992, we reached the minimum requirement of 25 PMI members building professionalism through project management, and, by early 1993, we had 42 PMI members, two-thirds of whom have joined PMI as a direct result of the prospective Arabian Gulf Chapter's organizational efforts.

In keeping with our Gulf-wide intentions, the first meeting of 1993 was held in the State of Bahrain on 21 January and 29 potential and registered members attended. Mr. Abdullah G. Al-Ghanim, senior vice president-engineering and project management, Saudi Aramco, spoke on Aramco's "Quality Improvement Program." The proposed constitution, bylaws and financial plans were presented in final draft form and discussed. An informal meeting was convened in Riyadh in late February 1993 to develop further interest in that area. This gathering was attended by the membership director, president, 8 other current members and 7 other interested professionals.

In March 3, 1993, the chapter application was submitted to the Vice President-Region I, Project Management Institute, in Vancouver, Canada, for the proposed Arabian Gulf Chapter of the Project Management Institute. In accordance with the bylaws, and upon review of the petition to form a local organization, the board of directors of the Project Management Institute presented the charter in March 1993.

PURPOSE

The Project Management Institute Arabian Gulf Chapter Mission (objective) is:
- To introduce and promote the advancement of the project management profession in the area and facilitate technical exchanges with PMI head office and other PMI Chapters on project management techniques, methods and current trends
- To provide a source of continuing professional development for members and others within the region
- To develop project management professionalism by providing stimulating, high-quality programs; and by providing a forum for regular interchange among professionals
- To build a strong continuing membership base of project management professionals by providing value-added membership services
- To advance the mission and objectives of the Project Management Institute within the Arabian Gulf Region.

ORGANIZATION

The Project Management Institute Arabian Gulf Chapter's organization consists of an elected board of president, vice president, treasurer, secretary, membership director.

ACTIVITIES

1994 was the third year of our chapter's life and was full of activities and achievements.

During that year, the chapter membership grew from 75 to 108 members. Also, a dedicated effort was exerted in expanding the chapter's activities throughout the major cities in the Gulf area such as Riyadh, Jeddah, Bahrain and Dubai.

The chapter membership growth was recognized by PMI International at the Annual Seminar/Symposium held at Vancouver, Canada, in October 1994. In recognition of its contribution, the Arabian Gulf Chapter was recognized as the Chapter of the Year in Region I, which includes geographical regions outside the United States. Also, during 1994, Chapter #57 conducted 8 dinner meetings (5 in Dhahran and one each in Riyadh, Jubail and Dubai). It was in Bahrain where we held the second annual conference on December 6–8, 1994.

We also launched a promotion program where the chapter's activities, goals and objective were introduced to the local business community and professionals, mainly in the eastern, central and western regions of Saudi Arabia. This included introduction letters and visits by active PMI members to selected firms and individuals. This promotion and awareness program achieved its goal, as evidenced by the number of companies that accepted to co-sponsor our monthly activities as well as the annual conference held at Bahrain.

Plans are being evaluated to establish specific committees to help the PMI-AGC Board in the areas of programs, membership, training, public relations.

Does your organization have established relations with agencies or departments of your government, or with universities? Please describe.

To date, we have no formal relations with such agencies. However, we have members in the local chapter and PMI International who are from government agencies such as PT&T, Royal Commission for Jubail and Yanbu, and universities.

Further, we have plans to establish joint efforts with other professional societies within the Gulf, such as the American Society of Civil Engineers.

The Global Status of the Project Management Profession

SOUTH AFRICA

STATUS OF THE PROJECT MANAGEMENT PROFESSION

In general, at what stage is the project management profession in your country today (i.e., newly introduced, growing, mature)? Please comment.

Project management has been used in South Africa for the last 20–25 years. The South Africa Chapter of PMI was established in 1961. Today project management is practiced in a wide range of industries at various maturity levels. The most rapid growth has been experienced in the information systems and financial services sectors. PMI has a collaborative agreement with the Computer Society of SA (4500 members) to promote project management in the information systems sector.

What industries or types of projects are the main users of modern project management in your country or region today?

In its formative years, project management in the architect, engineering and construction industries tended to follow the influence of the British professions while major projects undertaken in the petrochemical and minerals industry introduced the American philosophies. Today all these industries are using project management, as are the information systems, financial services, government, defense, communications, pharmaceutical, industries and others (i.e., the full cross-section covered by PMI's specific interest groups).

What industries or areas of application in your country have the greatest need for more or better project management? What industries or organizations offer the greatest opportunities for growth of professional project management in your country? Why?

The National Reconstruction and Development Program has generated an increased demand for improved ways of executing social and infrastructure projects. There is, however, a need for project management in all application areas. The backlog of infrastructure in the housing, electricity and telecommunications sectors offers significant growth opportunities. South Africa has a well-developed financial services sector, while the information systems sector continues to grow.

> We are very happy that most of the world finally opened for us and that we are not a stepchild any longer...South Africa is very much a part of the global trend, an awareness all over the world that project management is the new management philosophy—that you can use it in construction, pharmaceuticals, or to develop a greengrocer's shop—it's a universal concept...I want to make a prediction that the Global Forum, in years to come, will be one of the most important and significant events of the annual PMI Seminar/Symposium...
>
> Pieter Oosthuizen
> PMI-South Africa

How can the project management profession be most effectively advanced in your country?

Project management education and training within the framework of recognized national and international certification standards is becoming more accepted by the major organizations in the public and private sectors. This trend is accelerating due to the need to improve productivity to compete with the many global corporations now investing in the country. It is envisaged that the formation of an independent national Project Management Organization will provide the focal point for this growing profession. A fundamental goal for this national body is to provide a "home" for project management practitioners affiliated to all national and international project management organizations and other professional societies where project management has been identified as a specific area of interest.

What impact will globally recognized project management standards or certification have on the project management profession in your country?

Meaningful internationally accepted standards for certification will enhance and promote the image of the project management profession in all sectors of the economy. These standards will provide the reference point for the South African project management profession to contribute to the emerging standards required by the South African Qualifications Authority. These standards will also enable global corporations to recruit skilled project management resources to staff their investment projects and thus transfer technology and management skills more rapidly to their local staff.

ISSUES OF COMMON GLOBAL INTEREST

What should be contained in a global Project Management Body of Knowledge (PMBOK)?

A global Project Management Body of Knowledge (PMBOK) should address those areas common to all countries, such as multicultural issues, international contract and procurement methodologies, and communication issues.

How important will international "Standards" for project management be in your country or region? Please comment.

International Standards will enable regions, nations and individuals to benchmark their competencies against the level generally accepted by the global project management profession.

Is project management certification of interest in your country? What type of project management certification?

There is a widespread and growing interest in project management certification in all application areas. While PMI's PMP is the most prevalent for project management professionals, the certified project manager from the APM or similar is likely to become a desired standard for the superior project manger. At the national level the country would need to establish standards of equivalency that would recognize certification from other industry sectors, such as the Computer Society of South Africa who themselves have agreements with other national and international organizations.

What is your interest or position on a unified global project management association or organization? If you support such an organization, how should it be organized and for what objectives?

An international professional project management designation administered by a global project management organization is essential for universal recognition of the project management profession. Noting the limited volunteer resources available, this body should focus on priorities, the highest one being internationally recognized certification.

This certification should make provision for adaptation by different national bodies and industry sectors. An objective should be to unify the project management certification process across industries and countries.

How can project management associations around the world better communicate and cooperate to advance the project management profession?

Project management associations around the world must increasingly provide forums for communication and collaboration amongst individuals, nations and industry sectors. All electronic communication forms (e-mail, the Internet, World Wide Web, CompuServe, etc.) should be exploited to maximum advantage. Currently several home pages on the World Wide Web are providing an excellent service to the project management community.

YOUR ORGANIZATION

Briefly describe the history, purpose, organization and activities of the professional project management organization you represent.

The South Africa Chapter of the Project Management Institute was established in 1961. The Chapter has supported the PMP certification program since its inception in 1987 and to date has produced over 120 PMPs. The Chapter is centered in Johannesburg, and over the years members have gathered in the various centers, either informally or as formally constituted branches in various geographical regions.

The continuous decline of the value of the national currency has resulted in the Chapter operating a two-tier membership structure. Only some 20–30 percent of the 400 Chapter members are members of the International PMI body.

The South Africa Chapter is a respected member of Region I, for many years the only Chapter outside North America.

The Chapter has organized a Project Management Excellence Award for many years. The winner of this award has twice won the International Project of the Year award. In 1993 the Chapter discontinued their newsletter and formed an alliance with a commercial magazine focusing on the projects industry. The magazine publishes 6 times a year and enables news of the project management profession to reach a national readership of 6,000.

A national project management body will be launched in November 1995.

Does your organization have established relations with agencies or departments of your government, or with universities?

We have no formal relations with government bodies or agencies or universities. The Chapter is, however, represented in these bodies through its individual members. The Chapter is affiliated with the Association of Scientific and Technical Societies (AS&TS), the umbrella body for science and technology, and the Association of Management Institutes, a similar body representing insurance, banking, human resources, marketing, etc. More formal agreements with these organizations as well as other societies and institutions with a common interest in project management are viewed as significant opportunities for future growth.

SPAIN

STATUS OF PROJECT MANAGEMENT PROFESSION

In general, at what stage is the project management profession in your country today (i.e., newly introduced, growing, mature?) Please comment.

Growing.

What industries or types of projects are the main users of modern project management in your country or region today?

The majority of modern project management users are oil and gas engineering, military engineering, automotive industries, electronics/telecommunications, services, manufacturing industries, information technology and software development.

What industries or areas of application in your country have the greatest need for more or better project management? What industries or organizations offer the greatest opportunities for growth of professional project management in your country? Why?

No comment.

How can the project management profession be most effectively advanced in your country?

Until now we haven't had a project management organization. I believe we need to start one.

What impact will globally recognized project management standards or certification have on the project management profession in your country?

Unfortunately, no impact. Still, there are many people interested in it.

ISSUES OF COMMON GLOBAL INTEREST

What should be contained in a global Project Management Body of Knowledge (PMBOK)?

The core of a PMBOK should explain how a project must be managed, and it should contain information about project process management, procurement process management, quality project management, and design process management.

How important will international "Standards" for project management be in your country or region? Please comment.

International standards are a must in Spain. We believe international standards should reflect the needs of the project management profession. There are a lot of companies in Spain in the ISO 9000 certification process.

Is project management certification of interest in your country? What type of project management certification?

Yes. Until now we didn't have any type of project management certification, but we think that if we are able to create a Project Management Institute chapter, the situation in 1996 will change totally.

What is your interest or position on a unified global project management association or organization? If you support such an organization, how should it be organized and for what objectives?

Spain is very interested in creating and establishing a project management organization. We are very confident of the Project Management Institute, and we think that the Project Management Institute and other established organizations could assist us in setting up new associations in countries where these aspects are not yet developed.

How can project management associations around the world better communicate and cooperate to advance the project management profession?

Formalizing relations and maintaining regular communications and cooperation among national associations and possibly creating a common framework association could advance the project management profession.

YOUR ORGANIZATION

Briefly describe the history, purpose, organization and activities of the professional project management organization you represent.

We do not have a project management organization in Spain, but we need to create one.

Does your organization have established relations with agencies or departments of your government, or with universities?

No Response.

TURKEY

STATUS OF THE PROJECT MANAGEMENT PROFESSION

In general, at what stage is the project management profession in your country today (i.e., newly introduced, growing, mature)? Please comment.

Starting from the early eighties, project management has fast gained recognition in various Turkish industrial sectors as a new discipline aimed at improving the chances of successfully completing projects on time, within cost targets and by meeting performance criteria.

This was particularly true for the construction industry, which has shown remarkable growth from the late '70s on. While developing their financial, technical and managerial capabilities in a dynamic home market, a large number of construction firms have also entered foreign markets and succeeded in undertaking large-scale construction projects in North African and Middle Eastern countries. Lately, the new republics that have emerged from the former Soviet Union appear to be an important market with vast potential for many Turkish construction contractors. Some of them have already secured and successfully completed significant construction projects in some of these new republics and many are negotiating for new contracts. Turkey's geopolitical position and strong cultural ties in the region evidently support the rise of such business opportunities.

Similar developments in other industrial and service sectors have enabled the accumulation of substantial field experience in project management on one hand, and stimulated the demand for professionals with project management capabilities and training on the other.

What industries or types of projects are the main users of modern project management in your country or region today?

In Turkey, the following industries can be considered as potential users of modern project management techniques:
- Construction, particularly in tourist facilities, housing, infrastructure, highways, and industrial facility projects
- Telecommunications
- Manufacturing
- Auto
- Banking.

> [In] Turkey last month, I talked to a number of industry leaders, all of whom professed the need to have good project management education and good project management standards and practices ...these are lacking, except for those companies that go on the international scene and, to please overseas customers, import the people and the processes, and of course, once the project is done, those companies go back to their old ways. This is now changing. Major companies are beginning to feel the need to develop their own people. I can see nothing but good things happening in Turkey.
>
> Ahmet Taspinar
> PMI-Northern California

What industries or areas of application in your country have the greatest need for more or better project management? What industries or organizations offer the greatest opportunities for growth of professional project management in your country? Why?

In particular, industries with the greatest need for more and better project management are involved with significant large-scale domestic projects, and that have to compete with foreign companies in international markets. As explained above, the construction industry is a typical example. It therefore offers the greatest opportunity for the growth of professional project management in Turkey.

How can the project management profession be most effectively advanced in your country?

To have the project management profession advanced more effectively in Turkey, educational programs in this discipline first need to be expanded at both undergraduate and postgraduate levels at Turkish universities.

For example, the schools of architecture and civil engineering, which are the 2 main sources of construction professionals, are still chiefly "design-oriented" educational institutions. As also happens in many other countries, their graduates are educated to design the product rather than to manage the process. Although two post-graduate programs in Construction Management were started at Istanbul Technical University in the late '80s, the majority of architects and civil engineers still acquire management skills by on-the-job training or through foreign educational programs.

Second, "continuing education" programs need to be offered for practicing professionals, either by the universities or by professional organizations, to enhance and update their project management skills through formal and structured training.

What impact will globally recognized project management standards or certification have on the project management profession in your country?

Globally recognized project management standards or certification would definitely have an impact on the project management profession in a country if the companies from that country intend to compete for international projects in foreign and domestic markets. Otherwise, interest in adhering to such standards or seeking professional certification would not be expected to be high.

ISSUES OF COMMON GLOBAL INTEREST

What should be contained in a global Project Management Body of Knowledge (PMBOK)?

Since some processes and methods of managing projects differ somewhat from country to country, it is not easy to list what should be contained in a global Project Management Body of Knowledge. To build such a global PMBOK, project management professionals from different countries should perhaps question whether the PMI PMBOK drafted by the PMI Standards Committee could be used "as is" in their own country and suggest amendments wherever they feel it is necessary.

How important will international "Standards" for project management be in your country or region? Please comment.

As stated above, if a company intends to undertake projects in other countries, international standards for project management would be important. For example, when bidding for an international contract, a Turkish construction company definitely has to consider FIDIC specifications. Otherwise, local specifications issued by the Ministry of Public Works and Housing would be adequate.

Is project management certification of interest in your country? What type of project management certification?

We think that project management certification is of little interest in Turkey at the moment, because the advantages of being a "PMI-certified PMP" in Turkey are not yet clear to many project management professionals.

What is your interest or position on a unified global project management association or organization? If you support such an organization, how should it be organized and for what objectives?

In different countries of the world, when a profession gains some stature and recognition and national associations for that profession are founded, their coming together under the umbrella of one global association is a common trend that should, of course, be supported for project management associations too.

How can project management associations around the world better communicate and cooperate to advance the project management profession?

The means for communication and cooperation among project management associations around the world for advancing the project management profession would probably not differ much from those used by other professional associations. The first prerequisite, of course, is to set up a unified global project management association for that purpose. Holding international conferences at regular intervals, forming international working committees, starting a World Wide Web page and discussion lists on the Internet to establish a worldwide project management information network, and issuing copies of international (and essential national) project management standards, documents and forms on CD-ROM are a few additional ideas that might serve this purpose.

YOUR ORGANIZATION

Briefly describe the history, purpose, organization and activities of the professional project management organization you represent.

At the moment, a fully-organized PMI Chapter is not yet formed in Turkey, although some individual PMI members from Istanbul and Ankara have been recognized by PMI over the past 5 years.as Potential Chapter Sponsors. On the other hand, some project management professionals from Ankara are reportedly about to complete the legal procedures to set up a professional organization titled "Project Managers Association."

There are also a few private firms exclusively offering project management services in Turkey.

Does your organization have established relations with agencies or departments of your government, or with universities?

See "Briefly describe the history ..." above.

The Global Status of the Project Management Profession

UNITED KINGDOM

STATUS OF THE PROJECT MANAGEMENT PROFESSION

In general, at what stage is the project management profession in your country today (i.e., newly introduced, growing, mature)? Please comment.

The project management profession in the United Kingdom is well-developed and could be considered to be mature. Project management has been in the major project industries, e.g., engineering, construction and infrastructure, for many years and is extremely well defined and understood.

What industries or types of projects are the main users of modern project management in your country or region today?

Project management in the information technology and general business arena has developed over the last 5 years but has now reached a mature stage and is supported by a growing band of experienced project managers using appropriate tools and methods.

All industries in the United Kingdom are moving toward a management-by-project approach. There is no clear distinction between types of projects inasmuch as project management is being applied to small and large initiatives, low-cost and high-cost schemes, and sophisticated and relatively straightforward projects.

What industries or areas of application in your country have the greatest need for more or better project management? What industries or organizations offer the greatest opportunities for growth of professional project management in your country? Why?

Industries divide between those that follow a strict methodology in the information technology and general business areas and the more historical project-based industries that have a more intuitive approach to project management. I am not sure one could identify which industries have a greater need for more or better project management. All industries are improving their understanding and application of project management techniques. Probably the greatest change is the recognition of high-level input at the front end of the project and more attention to the interpersonal skills.

Particularly on internal projects, the needs to motivate and manage a team and to establish and ensure communications throughout the organization are essential. In the

> ● ● ● ● ● ● ● ● ● ● ●
> *... what we need to do, within this general environment of flourishing project management, is to continue to promote best-practice generic standards. What we don't want to do is to find people saying project management is an orange, or an apple, or project management is a state, or process. We want to say that* this *is what the standard of project management is. The way we can best do that is by having well-respected quality, practices, and professionalism that represent the discipline.*
> ● ● ● ● ● ● ● ● ● ● ●
> Peter W.G. Morris, APM

traditional project industries, where the client appoints a group of companies to design, develop, implement and hand over a facility, there is less need for the selling of either projects and the benefits of the project.

How can the project management profession be most effectively advanced in your country?

Project management can most effectively be advanced by making more people and organizations aware of the benefits of this approach and the fact that most, if not all, team-based working practices is indeed project management. People focusing on the wider range of skills necessary to successfully manage a project and then applying those skills would effectively advance the profession.

What impact will globally recognized project management standards or certification have on the project management profession in your country?

Globally recognized project management standards or certification would add value to the existing program. As the growth of multinational projects and mobility of labor increases, so the benefits of a transferable qualification expand. However, this is limited to a relatively small group of people, and the general acceptance, or indeed need, for global standards has not been determined.

ISSUES OF COMMON GLOBAL INTEREST

What should be contained in a global Project Management Body of Knowledge (PMBOK)?

The global Project Management Body of Knowledge can only identify high-level generic issues in project management. It is not possible to have a single detailed Body of Knowledge because all counties will develop and progress ideas in their own cultural style. Whilst the techniques and applications of project management may be universal, the detailed implementation and approach is a very personal issue.

How important will international "Standards" for project management be in your country or region? Please comment.

International standards of project management would be appropriate providing they are a framework or guideline. Again due to the variety of projects and clients, I do not believe it is feasible to impose a standard on how all projects should be managed. By their uniqueness and individuality the project management methods and approach must be tailored to a specific project.

Is project management certification of interest in your country? What type of project management certification?

Project management certification is of interest in the United Kingdom. A number of organizations are seeking certification programs and, in particular, demonstration of an individual's ability to manage projects or indeed play a very significant in the project team. The focus is clearly on an individual's ability, not on an individual's knowledge of project management issues.

What is your interest or position on a unified global project management association or organization? If you support such an organization, how should it be organized and for what objectives?

I was personally involved in the initial meeting for the global Project Management Association. I believe that the main benefit of a global federation is to agree on standards of reciprocity of membership. It would also enable information on developments of project management to be swiftly exchanged between countries so that the art and science of project management can be developed at an even faster pace.

The organization could be on either formal or informal. The important thing is to ensure that all countries have an equal say and right to contribute to the development. Its main objective must be for the mutual benefit of all members.

How can project management associations around the world better communicate and cooperate to advance the project management profession?

To ensure greater communication and cooperation all project management associations should respect the ideas and geographic boundaries of other project management associations. The important thing is for organizations to collaborate and not develop into a confrontational attitude over promoting different ideas of standards and programs. With a clear spirit of understanding and cooperation, communications could then be established by means of electronic network and regular, i.e., annual or biannual, high-level meetings. Possibly national associations could naturally form into geographical divisions, and each could elect a member to represent them in a global forum.

YOUR ORGANIZATION

Briefly describe the history, purpose, organization and activities of the professional project management organization you represent.

The APM Group Limited is the trading arm of the Association of Project Managers (established in 1972). The APM Group Limited was established in 1992 with a clear purpose of promoting the use of project management and providing advice and support to clients and practitioners alike. We provide a whole host of services ranging from advice on Professional Indemnity Insurance, training programs, recruitment service, development of ideas, methods and general promotion of the profession.

Does your organization have established relations with agencies or departments of your government, or with universities? Please describe.

We have established relations with a wide range of universities, agencies and government departments of all types. We also have an extensive network of over 150 companies, which either provide or buy in project management services that represent the leading thinkers of project management in the United Kingdom.

The Global Status of the Project Management Profession

UNITED STATES

STATUS OF THE PROJECT MANAGEMENT PROFESSION

In general, at what stage is the project management profession in your country today (i.e., newly introduced, growing, mature)? Please comment.

Project management has been in use in the United States for decades. Historically, project managers came from the construction (engineering) and defense industries. Project management is beginning to be recognized as a profession. Managing by projects, managing through projects, and managing entire corporations on the basis of projects is at various growth stages, depending on the industry.

What industries or types of projects are the main users of modern project management in your country or region today?

Construction/engineering, defense/aerospace, and pharmaceutical are probably the most developed industries using project management in the United States. Information management and movement (telecommunications), information systems, financial services, gas and electric utilities, manufacturing, and environmental industries are rapidly growing in their use of project management. Within the Project Management Institute, construction is the most represented industry (16.9 percent), followed by information systems (15.2 percent).

> ● ● ● ● ● ● ● ● ● ● ● ●
> … What is the potential for project management? One statistic that I have is that Microsoft Project has sold well over a million copies; that means that even if every member of PMI had a copy of MS Project, we could have covered only about 1.7 percent of the marketplace! …project management offers a common language within a company, an industry, a country, or the world … it is a communication medium.
> ● ● ● ● ● ● ● ● ● ● ● ●
> *Roger Glaser, PMI*

What industries or areas of application in your country have the greatest need for more or better project management? What industries or organizations offer the greatest opportunities for growth of professional project management in your country? Why?

Based on membership data from PMI, the industries with the greatest growth percentage are telecommunications (47.9 percent), financial services (25.5 percent), real estate/insurance (24.3 percent) and information systems (23.3 percent). Business management, health/human services, public administration/government, oil/gas/coal and most manufacturing industries (i.e., automotive, machinery, electronic, food, plastics and wood) are offering new opportunities for the growth of professional project management.

How can the project management profession be most effectively advanced in your country?

The advancement of the project management profession will depend largely on the perceived and actual benefits realized by major corporations and institutions, including government. Marketing efforts will need to be increased to create the awareness of project management's benefits. The downsizing, rightsizing and flattening of corporations and institutions is pushing project management to new levels of recognition. Continued efforts to develop a standardized or template approach to project management must be strengthened. Project management education, both institutional and professional, must also be strengthened.

What impact will globally recognized project management standards or certification have on the project management profession in your country?

Globally recognized project management standards will be critical for global corporations. Certification to ensure that standards are recognized, and that the recognized standards are being implemented, will be highly regarded. Thus, the profession of project management in the United States will be more widely recognized with certification a mandatory requirement for many major corporations.

ISSUES OF COMMON GLOBAL INTEREST

What should be contained in a global Project Management Body of Knowledge (PMBOK)?

A global PMBOK must contain the essence of project management knowledge and experience—the information people need when they're involved in the formal management of projects. The PMBOK should also address interpersonal skills required to organize and lead a project team, the specific skills needed to plan and control the project, and a general management philosophy. Cultural approaches need to be considered in some format.

How important will international "Standards" for project management be in your country or region? Please comment.

The requirement for project management standards is being demanded by more corporations as project management techniques and tools are implemented in their organizations. PMI has been informed (though not substantiated) that specific corporations within the United States have required Project Management Professional certification from those responding to Requests for Proposal. It only seems natural that International Standards (when established) will be required by international organizations.

Is project management certification of interest in your country? What type of project management certification?

More than 1,100 applicants were scheduled to take the PMI's Project Management Professional certification examination on June 16th, a 35 percent increase over the same period last year. There is significant and rapidly growing interest in this knowledge-based certification. Requests to develop a competency-based certification have also been increasing.

What is your interest or position on a unified global project management association or organization? If you support such an organization, how should it be organized and for what objectives?

A global project management organization would need to hold the core intellectual property of the project management profession, i.e., the standards and certification process. However, no one country can be aware of the cultural differences that exist between countries. Thus, each country should be represented within this global organization and have the discretion to adapt cultural requirements into the project management standards that require such attention (e.g., contract negotiation), but not to the extent that changes will be at variance to the standards. Each country should also have the ability to customize, within specified parameters, the qualifying requirements of certification. There should, however, be an executive body overseeing these customizations. To prevent global confusion, a system should be established to indicate the country in which the practicing project manager has achieved certification.

How can project management associations around the world better communicate and cooperate to advance the project management profession?

Technology has allowed communication to flow with relative ease and low cost. The Internet offers great potential for the exchange of information directly between associations and in project management forums. Cooperative agreements between associations allow for the exchange of ideas and partnering initiatives and should be encouraged. Global forums, such as this one, will also help unify the profession. Cooperative educational endeavors must also be encouraged.

YOUR ORGANIZATION

Briefly describe the history, purpose, organization and activities of the professional project management organization you represent.

Established in 1969, the Project Management Institute is an international, nonprofit professional organization dedicated to advancing the state-of-the-art in the management of projects. Membership is open to any person or entity interested in furthering the purposes of the Institute. The board of directors is responsible for the actions of PMI. The board is primarily a policy making body made up of volunteers, either through election or appointment. Elected officers include the Chair of the Board of Directors, President, Vice President-Technical Activities, Vice President-Public Relations, Vice President-Administration, Vice President-Region I, Vice President-Region II, Vice President-Region III, and four Ex-Officios. Appointed board members include the Executive Director, Publisher/Editor-in-Chief, Director of Certification, Director of Educational Services, Director of Standards, and Director of Seminar/Symposium. Standing Committees include Accreditation, Awards, Certification, Education, Ethics, Information Systems Advisory Committee, Intersociety Liaison, Marketing, Nominations, *Project Management Journal* Editorial Review Board, Professional Development Group, Publications Board, Research and Development Committee, Standards, and Strategic Planning. Other official governing bodies include the Council of Chapter Presidents and the Specific Interest Group Council. The day-to-day operation of the Institute is under the management of the Executive Director.

Activities provide member benefits that focus on skills and knowledge improvement at local, industry, regional, and international levels—networking with peers at local chapters; access to a common area of interest in an industry or function through Specific Interest Groups; learning about the state-of-the-art of project management at the Annual Seminar/Symposium; acquiring knowledge at regional workshops; and gaining educational and professional recognition through the PMP Certification program. Publications add to skills and knowledge improvement and include the monthly magazine, *PM Network,* the quarterly *Project Management Journal,* and access to numerous discounted books and handbooks that add to the project management knowledge base.

Does your organization have established relations with agencies or departments of your government, or with universities? Please describe.

In April 1995, PMI and the U.S. Army Corps of Engineers entered into a Partnering Agreement, which declared a public affirmation of both organizations' commitment to project planning and control to achieve efficient, cost effective and timely project completion. A similar agreement is pending with the U.S. Department of Energy.

As part of its commitment to the educational system, PMI has an accreditation process that seeks to review the content and process of project management education in graduate and professional schools to assure that students who study project management will have the educational background to effectively serve modern society within this field. PMI continues to foster growth in project management courses through undergraduate and continuing education programs.

PMI has also entered into 12 cooperative agreements with other countries and associations to foster its mission of "... building professionalism in project management ..." These organizations are AACE International, Australian Institute of Project Management, Automotive Industry Action Group, Center for Excellence in Project Management, Construction Management Association of America, Engineering Advancement Association of Japan, Institute of Industrial Engineers, International Project Management Association, Performance Management Association, Korean Institute of Project Management and Technology, Russian Project Management Association, and Western Australian Project Management Association.

VENEZUELA

STATUS OF THE PROJECT MANAGEMENT PROFESSION

In general, at what stage is the project management profession in your country today (i.e., newly introduced, growing, mature)? Please comment.

The project management profession in Venezuela is growing in a very important way. The Venezuela Chapter, centered in Caracas, has a very high level of interest from many industrial sectors, both private and public. The potential membership and resource base is very promising, and we look forward to very shortly becoming a key part of PMI's Region I.

Venezuela has a population of about 22 million and the Caracas metropolitan area has about 4–5 million persons. Caracas is the headquarters of several large, world-class oil and petrochemical companies such as Lagoven, Maraven, Corpoven and Pequiven, as well as the umbrella organization for these companies, PDVSA.

In addition, Venezuela has many engineering consulting companies of which the largest are affiliated in varying degrees with U.S. and/or European engineering companies. These affiliated companies, e.g., Kellogg, Bechtel, Fluor Daniel, Foster Wheeler, have many PMI members assigned to Caracas and other parts of Venezuela from time to time.

Further, many non-petroleum sector companies who employ project management principles and have knowledgeable professionals have headquarters in Caracas. Procter & Gamble, Latin America is a prime example of a company who has both Venezuelan professionals as well as expatriate project management professionals in its organization.

> ● ● ● ● ● ● ● ● ● ● ● ●
>
> We are trying to sell the idea of project management in Venezuela, the idea that project management is a *profession*, not a position. Part of the problem is in translating the term "project manager" into Spanish; we have no word for management to [distinguish it as] a profession, rather than a specific position in a company…
>
> ● ● ● ● ● ● ● ● ● ● ● ●
>
> Lorenzo Caldentey, PMI

A further consideration is the unique situation of Caracas in Venezuela. It is "the center" of most project management activity in the country. Professionals in other cities such as Maracaibo, Barquisimeto, Puerto La Cruz and Valencia frequently visit their headquarters in Caracas and undoubtedly would be involved at some level in the Venezuela Chapter located in Caracas.

What industries or types of projects are the main users of modern project management in your country or region today?

See "What industries or areas of application …" below.

What industries or areas of application in your country have the greatest need for more or better project management? What industries or organizations offer the greatest opportunities for growth of professional project management in your country? Why?

Venezuela actually has a labor force of about 10 million. About 8 million of the population is less than 18 years old.

The PDVSA and affiliate companies' "Expansion Plan (1994–2002)" has a specific target, among others, to increase the oil production levels from 2.8 million barrels per day up to 4.0 million barrels per day. Some strategic joint ventures have been formed between national and international companies that are recognized worldwide in the oil business, for exploring the oil-inactive fields and heavy-crude oil extra heavy-crude oil reservoirs. Their investments are estimated to be about 40 billion US$: 60 percent a shared contribution by PDVSA and 40 percent by other partners. At this point, some investments are still needed to increase the refining capacity and petrochemical production levels. The items discussed above means putting large projects into effect that will involve national and international companies that are important in the oil sector. Some of these companies are PDVSA, Lagoven, Maraven, Corpoven, Pequiven, Teikoku Oil, British Petroleum, Shell, Exxon, Mitsubishi, Total of France, Texaco, Inelectra, Tenoconsult, Tecnofluor, Fluor Daniel, Foster Wheeler, Otepi, Vepica, Jantesa, CIT Harris, Kellogg, Betchel, Tripoliven, and many others.

The chemical sector will continue its increase, through the initiatives of local and foreign private companies and by forces from the petrochemical sector to which it is connected.

In this broad sector, we can gather companies from the following industries: chemistry, agricultural chemistry, plastic resins, plastic, coloring matters/pigments, painting/enamel, and others. This area of commerce made a gross income of 150,000 millions of Bs. on sales in 1993, and it is expected to put multiple projects into effect, including research and improving the quality of its products. The following companies are outstanding or prominent: Tripolven, Corimon, Grupo Quimico, Polimeros del Zulia, Plasticos Lagos, BASF, Pinco Pittsburgh, Montana, Ferro, Shell, Quimica de Venezuela, and others.

The demand for energy foreseen by the year 2010 involves continuous realization of large investments to increase the capacity to produce hydroelectric energy. The construction of the hydroelectric centers, Uribante-Caparo and Macagua II, will be concluded; the construction of the hydroelectric center, Caruechi, begun. Construction of the hydroelectric center, Tocoma, will begin later. Also projects will continue to be put into effect to improve and make the systems of transmission and distribution of electric power more efficient. In this sector, the following companies are outstanding: Edelca, Elecar, Cadafe, Enelven, as well as some of the engineering consultant firms, equipment manufacturers, and construction companies that actively participate, including Asea Brown Boveri, Asincro, Deproex, Dell'Acqua, Mannesmann Rexrroth, Geohidra, Commetasa, Imosa, Waagner Biro, Hilmave, GPI, Consorcio la Llovizna, Marubeni, and others. It is worth mentioning that several of these companies maintain work connections with multinational companies.

The development of tourism has strengthened the construction sector, and housing construction projects will continue to be put into effect. In the future there are projects to build a railway to improve the communications and internal transportation of the country. It has been planned to make a network of underground transportation in the city of Caracas, with the progressive incorporation of 3 additional channels. The companies that constitute the cement and concrete industries have reached a gross sale of 40,000 millions of Bs. It is planned to put some projects into effect to increase the production of these plants.

Among the companies that make up the "iron, steel, and metallurgical" sector, whose sales fluctuated close to 450,000 millions Bs. in 1993, a power increase and some expansion of plants has been foreseen.

In the computer sector we can observe an increase that has been maintained over a long period of time. Sales in this area have been estimated at 40,000 millions of Bs. in 1993. In relation to the growth of software and systems information, sales were greater than 10,000 millions Bs. in 1993. In this sector many nationally and internationally recognized enterprises take part, including consulting firms like IBM, Summa Corporation, Unisys, Siemens, Nixdorf, Microsoft of Venezuela, Manapro, Andersen Consulting, Espineira Sheldon and Price Waterhouse, Novellco, Rodin Software Applications, Electronic Data Systems, Apple Computer and Plus Systems and Ernst & Young-Perez, Mena & Evert & Morales, among others.

Because of the accelerated growth in telecommunications that was started by the privatization of the public telephone company (CANTV) in 1991, we now see new levels of confidence in relation to investments and realization of projects for the period of 1994–2005. The investment made by CANTV alone in the year 1991 was more than 64 millions of dollars, and it increased to more than a billion dollars by 1992–1993. Amongst the areas of growth, in the present and in the future, we can distinguish basic telephone, wireless telephone, public telephone, intelligent telephone, digitalization and complex systems of telecommunications. Amongst others, the following companies are outstanding: CANTV, Siemens, Ericcson, NEC, AT&T, Telenorma, Movilnet, Telcel.

Another sector that will keep on realizing projects in the creation of new products, improvement of the quality of the existing products, scientific research, raising the capacity of production, and overhauling existing plants, is the pharmaceutical and cosmetic industry and the detergent and hygiene industry. This area of business made a gross sale in 1993 of approximately 100,000 million Bs. Amongst others, we have the following outstanding companies: Hoechst, Bayer, Ciba-Geigy, Sandoz, Abbot, Behrens, Procter & Gamble, Avon, Colgate-Palmolive, Revlon, Pfizer, Gillette, Bristol Myers, Warner-Lambert and Johnson & Johnson.

It is important to point out the development of human resources in the country through training, learning and specialization; "the biggest competitive advantage depends on the capacity of the technological institutes." Institutes of management development continue to improve human resources. We should make a special mention of the Universidad Catolica Andres Bello, which has opened studies for postgraduate students in "Project Management of Engineering" and Universidad Central de Venezuela and Universidad Simon Bolivar for its specializations and magister in management, University Metropolitan for their magister status in management in construction and the Instituto de Estudios Superiores de Administracion, IESA for its specialization and research in the field of management.

How can the project management profession be most effectively advanced in your country?

Just by continuing to insist on project management professionalism, mainly done by the Venezuelan Chapter through its presentations, programs and courses.

What impact will globally recognized project management standards or certification have on the project management profession in your country?

Up to this moment we have had only one exam. Twenty-one people took the exam and nine of them obtained the PMP certificate. Most of them were from one consulting firm. The other consulting firms are making their own arrangements so that they can prepare their people to become PMPs. In the future certification will become more and more important, and from now on we are preparing to give the exam at every opportunity.

ISSUES OF COMMON GLOBAL INTEREST

What should be contained in a global Project Management Body of Knowledge (PMBOK)?

We have no comments to make on changes to the content of the PMBOK. Our only advice would be in the direction of its translation to other languages, especially to Spanish. It should be done so that you have both versions, English and Spanish, side by side, since there are many terms and their translation is not the same in the different Spanish-speaking countries. The PMP exam should also have the questions in both languages.

How important will international "Standards" for project management be in your country or region? Please comment.

See "Is project management certification ..." below.

Is project management certification of interest in your country? What type of professional project management certification?

Up to this moment it is not important at all. As time goes on there will become a real need. The type and standards should be those now applied in the United States.

What is your interest or position on a unified global project management association or organization? If you support such an organization, how should it be organized and for what objectives?

See "How can project management associations ..." below.

How can project management associations around the world better communicate and cooperate to advance the project management profession?

We see PMI today as an international organization. We think that it sounds perfect that every member is part of only one organization and then the group of people that live in a geographical location will work together in a chapter of the global organization. We really think that way is better than to have local organizations that come together in a kind of federation. If we are all a part of the same thing, we will all defend it. If it is necessary or looks nicer to change the PMI into IPMA, International Project Management Institute, we think it can be done. The PMP certificate would have an international sense and would be accepted all over the world.

YOUR ORGANIZATION

Briefly describe the history, purpose, organization and activities of the professional project management organization you represent.

There is not too much that can be said. Our chapter is one year old and we feel that we did quite a good job. We have about 100 members, we have done 8 programs, 2 seminars, 2 courses to prepare for the PMP exam, one PMP exam. In every program we had more than 100 people in attendance and in the last one we had 217. We are about to have the annual assembly, where we will decide about our new board. We are completely sure that the potential in Venezuela for the project management profession is enormous and we are trying to be the driving force that will make that a reality.

Does your organization have established relations with agencies or departments of your government, or with universities? Please describe.

We have relations mainly with the oil companies, the consulting firms, and the Universidad Catolica Andres Bello.

PART II
PRESENTATIONS BY DISTINGUISHED SPEAKERS

PRESENTATIONS BY DISTINGUISHED SPEAKERS

Introduction by David L. Pells

THE MATURATION AND development of the project management profession in various regions of the world are significant, reflecting the growing recognition of the importance of project management as an effective approach to achieving economic objectives. Globalization of the profession however, requires countries and organizations in various parts of the world to work together for common goals. This, in turn, requires leadership skills and a broad understanding of issues facing the project management profession around the world.

The first Global Project Management Forum in New Orleans featured speeches by distinguished leaders of the project management profession from around the world. These specially invited speakers, whose presentations are contained in this section, include leaders of the world's largest and most influential professional project management associations, including PMI, IPMA (Europe), APM (Great Britain), ENAA (Japan), SOVNET (Russia) and experts, including Paul Dinsmore (Brazil), Alan Stretton (Australia), and Robert Youker (USA) were invited to add perspective from other parts of the world and from the World Bank.

These individuals are not only true project management experts, but they also have broad experience and perspective related to transnational, multicultural, and globalization-related issues confronting the project management profession today. As these speeches in New Orleans demonstrated, they also share a common vision of closer cooperation, project management as a truly global profession, and the project management profession as a global resource now available to the people and organizations around world who are badly in need of such expertise.

These speakers also offered challenges, not the least of which is the challenge to overcome communication barriers. By bringing representatives together from around the world to meet face-to-face, to discuss issues of both commonality and disagreement, and to listen to experts with global perspectives, perhaps the Global Forum in New Orleans was a major step forward in lowering communication barriers.

It was an honor and a great pleasure for me to introduce each of these speakers at the first Global Forum in New Orleans. I am again honored to introduce their speeches to you on the pages that follow.

PROJECT MANAGEMENT: AN INTERNATIONAL PROFESSION

Peter Morris
Chair, Association of Project Managers (United Kingdom)

I have been asked to speak on project management as an international profession. I thought for a long time about whether or not to put a question mark at the end of my title. Does my paper question whether there *should* or *could* be an international profession; or does it assert and describe one which *exists*? In the end I decided to leave off the question mark, preferring, out of conviction, to suggest that it exists, if only perhaps in preliminary form—and such is indeed the case. But in reality there are many questions as to the viability of project management as an international profession and it is these which I wish principally to address.

The discipline

That there is a recognized discipline of project management—or as I would prefer it, "the management of projects"—I have no doubt. I can identify, so far, three periods in the evolution of the discipline, each, curiously, about 15 years long.

The first was the period of formation that occurred between 1955 and 1970. This was the period when virtually all project management techniques were invented. Nearly all of them were developed by the U.S. defense-aerospace community (DoD and NASA)—network scheduling (PERT), earned value analysis, configuration management, value engineering, work breakdown structures, etc. (Construction had its contribution with CPM and Precedence but really surprisingly little else.) The motive at this time was primarily engineering management—schedule urgency and engineering difficulty. The threat was the Russians. Projects and project management operated largely in a "closed system" environment, shielded from the pressures of society, funding and ecology. The Apollo Man-on-the-Moon program was the archetype of this era.

In 1969 this changed. Vietnam, the OPEC embargo, and the environmental movement all rose rapidly and dramatically to constrain projects and their management across a wide range of industries—defense/aerospace oil, power, transportation, etc. For the next 15 years—until the mid '80s—project management was to grow progressively into new areas of application largely on the backs first of high-tech industries (propelled significantly by NATO) but also through the encouragement of consultants and other enthusiasts. Not least amongst this latter group were the professional project management societies, primarily PMI and Internet (now IPMA), both founded in the late '60s/early '70s. (APM was founded at exactly this time, initially as the U.K. Chapter of Internet.) This second era of project management was one of growth.

Two notable features of this era were (a) that the concepts, tools and techniques being used were almost entirely those of the 1955–70 period and (b) that the failure rate of many projects (and almost all those whose data is in the public record) was very high. Projects typically came in over budget, often late and they did not necessarily perform as intended. Further, the reasons for this poor performance were as often as not to be found in poor project definition and/or the impact of external factors, yet both these major areas of attention were virtually ignored entirely during this period. Project management was in reality inadequately defined and insufficiently practiced.

The mid '80s saw several major changes which were to have a huge impact on the discipline.

- Total Quality emerged as a comprehensive and revolutionary view of management, emphasizing attention to the customer, continuous improvement, teamwork, and management by fact throughout the (project) life cycle.
- Financial engineering became significantly more important—certainly in public sector projects (e.g., Build-Operate-Transfer) but in fact in most project sectors.
- Environmental issues became inescapably of prime significance, whether conceptually as for example in addressing the concept of sustainability, or very practically in terms of meeting health or safety issues, pollution, or Environmental Impact Assessments Requirements.
- Technology began to make huge impacts on the way we manage projects. User friendly (4GL) computing only really emerged in the '80s; Windows, interoperability, CAE/CALS, EDI etc., are now really changing project management practices.
- And lastly (perhaps) the proper roles of the project sponsor and owner began to become better articulated and systematized.

Crucially, our view of project management is no longer the essentially closed system one of before. It is more holistic. The old definition of project management's realm as being delivering the project "on time, in budget, to technical specification" is increasingly being recognized as inadequate. Today's objectives are all about achieving project success, about delivering customer value, shortening time-to-market, optimizing performance, and so on. This has been the era of project management maturity[1].

Project management is now practiced by thousands of managers; recognized as important to institutional success by leaders worldwide; and increasingly taught by universities. We are even moving towards agreement on what constitutes the standard project management body of knowledge.

Yet, can we say that project management is truly widely understood in the sense that corporate planning or human resource management is? And do we really have a clearly articulated view on whether it is—or need be—a profession, in the same way, for example, that medicine, law, architecture and engineering are?

What actually is a profession? What does it mean to be a professional?

Essentially, a professional is someone who has achieved a recognized level of competency in his or her field and is hence able to practice independently. This generally means that:

- There is a body of knowledge recognized in the profession domain.

- The practitioner has the requisite education and training and has demonstrated that he or she has the knowledge needed to practice competently.
- Certain standards of practice and ethics of behavior are recognized and subscribed to.
- The professional practitioner demonstrates knowledge, judgment and skills in the execution of his or her work.
- Certain levels of competent performance are expected of the member of the profession, this usually being assessed on the basis (a) of a demonstration that the professional has the requisite knowledge of the subject and (b) can demonstrate appropriate practical experience of its practice.

Recognition of the right to belong to a profession, subject to the above rules, administered by the relevant professional body, allows one then to practice independently rather than necessarily under someone else's direct supervision.

And, incidentally, society needs to recognize as valid the professional body that sets these standards and rules and that tests, admits and regulates its members' rights to practice.

Does this sound appropriate to project management? It is "necessary" to have a demonstration of project management competence like this in order to practice?

I believe the answer is no—and yes. I cannot envisage the day when managers, as managers, will have to be recognized by their professional society in order to manage. That just is not the way the real world is. The Chairman of AT&T does not have to demonstrate that he has passed the requirements of a management professional in order to manage AT&T.

Professionalism becomes more relevant when the domain is relatively clearly bounded, the technical knowledge required is significant, and liability for inadequate performance is serious and can be clearly reduced by strong competency-based regulation. Frankly that often only pertains weakly to project management.

Yet there is undoubtedly a demand for some demonstration of project management competency, and for all of the characteristics of professionalism that have just been outlined. This demand comes from several different groups. It comes from practitioners who feel they have a skill and want it recognized; from graduates looking to work in project management who are not going into one of the other professions; from companies selling project management services wishing to demonstrate that their staff have attained a recognized level of competency; and from purchasers of project management services wishing similarly for some external validation of the competency of the people they will be employing.

So I think we can say that professionalism in project management is without doubt appropriate. And that, while professional qualifications in project management may not always be necessary, they are generally clearly desirable.

Should the project management competency qualifications to some extent be industry-specific? After all, many would argue that the project management competencies needed to manage a missile project are different from those of a building project, likewise a new pharmaceutical drug from a new software program. The idea has substance, but beware: making the qualification too industry-specific weakens project management as a generic, cross-industry discipline. We might note however that many examples of industry specific project management qualifications already exist. In the U.K., for example, all the vocational qualifications—NVQs—are industry-specific.

Existing project management professional qualifications

Most people would probably say that there are two sets of professional project management qualifications currently being promoted and used: one in project management and the other for project managers. Of the former, PMI's PMP is without doubt the most established. Qualifications similar to the PMP exist in Germany, France, the U.K. and Australia.

An important issue for such qualifications is the extent to which they have a competency assessment. The PMP has next to no requirement of evidence of work-ased competency. The Australian is very competency-orientated.

The only qualification at the project manager level is APM's Certificated Project Manager (CPM) qualification. This is now being adopted by IPMA. The project management qualifications generally require only evidence of basic, albeit fairly comprehensive, knowledge of the project management body of knowledge. (Several project management bodies of knowledge currently exist[2] with work proceeding on a global BOK.[3]) These have varying requirements of work-based competency; the CPM qualifications on the other hand are much more demanding. Thus APM's/IPMA's Certificated Project Manager requires a 5,000-word paper on a significant project or projects on which the applicant was project manager; references by the candidate's client and/or manager; and an interview conducted by two CPMs, one of whom must be from the candidate's industry sector, designed to test his or her knowledge and experience.

A very important point is accreditation: that is, who gives anyone (any organization) the right to issue professional qualifications. It is my suspicion that this issue has not been thought through sufficiently yet for many or even most of the project management qualifications. Professional organizations in the U.K. have historically been "accredited" when they obtain Royal Charter status (assuming they seek this, which APM is not doing). Alternatively, accreditation may be given by UKAS—the U.K. Accreditation Service. To the extent possible, APM would like to see IPMA providing accreditation of national qualifications.

International collaboration and validation

For some time there has been talk of various of these qualifications being adopted by different nations. To a considerable extent this is already happening. Many people from different countries have already taken, and been awarded, the PMP qualification. In effect, several countries, for example South Africa and Canada, having PMI Chapters as their only national project management professional associations, are offering the PMP as their countries' project management qualification. The CPM, insofar as it has been adopted by IPMA, is also a project management qualification available in several different countries.

Yet it would be a mistake I believe—as do my colleagues on the Council of APM—to expect standard qualifications such as the PMP and CPM to be de facto international qualifications. The reason is a combination of language, culture, and the acceptability of the bodies of knowledge on which the qualifications are based. While there may be groups of countries that have a shared view of project management, worldwide it is simply unrealistic to expect all the different nations to understand and accept a common definition of project management (and all its attributes), which would be implied by a truly international set of project management qualifications. The Germans see project management concepts and definitions subtly differently from the Arabs; the Japanese from the Russians; the Americans from the Australians.

The desire to proselytize and to be influential internationally is not only natural, it is generally beneficial. But in the end we would do well to recognize our national differences.

The future that I see is not one of a very small number of project management qualifications adopted by a large number of different countries. (Nor is it one of just one or two project management professional societies setting the professional standards of education, training, examinations, values, ethics, work-based competency standards, and so on.) I see a multi-polar project management world, with the various national societies having their own project management professional qualification requirements.

But what I also see is a need for a body operating a the international level to calibrate and coordinate the professional standards of different national project management societies. And the organization I personally see as the most suited to this role is IPMA.

IPMA is not comparable to PMI. PMI exists primarily as a professional society for its members. APM and the other IPMA national societies do the same. But IPMA itself does not. IPMA currently runs some international events (congresses, seminars, etc.), facilitates communication between project management bodies, and provides a small number of services. It is not in the business of recruiting individual members. It is not even in the business of issuing standards for project knowledge, experience, values, ethics, competency, and exams, *which would be operated at the national level.* (The Global BOK that IPMA has now begun work on is in effect a meta-BOK—a high-level BOK under which the national BOKs would sit.[3]

With dozens of countries having dozens of slightly different project management standards, what there is a need for is an international calibration and coordination body. Someone who can say that the Korean BOK, or the British or Czech, is not out of line with what the discipline would recognize. And that the professional qualifications being offered by different countries also compare. Indeed, a PMP, Projektfachmann (Germany's PMP), or APMP (the UK's) qualification that was validated (accredited) by IPMA would be enormously valuable. It would show this national qualification is accepted by the worldwide project management professional body. It would be a major step towards internationally transportable project management qualifications.

Of course, the activities of IPMA need not be limited solely to validation of national project management qualifications. There is a need for such a body to organize expert seminars and conferences, and to provide an advisory secretariat.

I say IPMA. There may be many who say, why not PMI? I strongly support PMI (I have been a member since 1977.) Yet PMI is really a national association; or insofar as there is PMI Canada, South Africa, New Zealand, etc., PMI comprises both regional chapters and national societies. IPMA is not like PMI. IPMA comprises national project management societies. Its mission is to promote project management through collaboration and coordination of the national associations' activities. Its natural role is, I believe, as I have outlined it above.

Conclusion

The professional project management societies have been in existence now for about 25 years. Never has interest in project management been greater or the outlook better. There is strong growth in most countries, and interest in international collaboration.

But despite our 25 years, we should recognize that we are still relatively young and in some ways inexperienced as professionals. As I have argued, the motives and modalities of project management professionalism are in some areas still unclear. We have much to do in establishing ourselves as professionals even in our own countries.

Internationally, we have a real opportunity. Very few professions indeed have their qualifications coordinated and validated by supra-national body. The model that I have proposed here is realistic, meets practical needs, and adds significant value to the national qualifications.

Let us, the national societies, recognize the level to which we really belong—the national level. Let us keep clear the distinctions between an international project management calibrating and coordinating body and the national awarding bodies.

I look forward to meeting again after the next 25 years to review the progress towards professionalism on which we are now embarking!

References
1. This historical background is described in detail in my book *The Management of Projects*, Thomas Telford, 1994, available through PMI Publications.
2. Wirth D. and Tryloff D.E. "Preliminary comparison of six efforts to document the project management body of knowledge" *International Journal of Project Management* Vol. 13(2) pp109-118 1995.
3. See J. Rodney Turner, "International Project Management Association: Global Qualification, certification and accreditation," *International Journal of Project Management* Vol. 14 (1), pp. 1–6, 1996.

Peter W. G. Morris, Ph.D., is a director of Bovis Ltd., one of the largest construction companies in the world, with responsibility for Special Projects. During 1984–1989, Morris was on the faculty of Oxford University, where he continues as an Associate Fellow of Templeton College and as a faculty member. He is currently Chairman of the Association of Project Managers. Prior to his work at Oxford, Morris was responsible for the international program management activities of Arthur D. Little, an international consulting company based in Cambridge, Mass., USA. He is the author of over 45 papers and chapters in books, as well as two books, The Anatomy of Major Projects (John Wiley & Sons, Chichester, 1987) and The Management of Projects (Thomas Telford, London, 1994).

GLOBAL ISSUES: THE PROJECT MANAGEMENT INSTITUTE'S VIEW

Kent Crawford, PMP
Chair, PMI Board of Directors

WELCOME TO THE global Project Management Forum. This is an historic event, which I believe we will come to view as a milestone in the globalization of the profession of project management.

We are faced with the opportunity to affect the world like no other profession. I am honored to be a part of this group of distinguished representatives. We represent a widely diverse set of viewpoints, opinions and biases. It's important for us to recognize these differences, discuss the issues openly, and work together to build the profession.

Building the profession: I believe that is why we are here today. Project management is the career of this decade and of the 21st century.

In previous decades, our economies have focused on performance in manufacturing and other areas of industry. But recently, a tremendous surge of interest is occurring in increasing the effectiveness of design, development and implementation in a variety of areas including not only the traditional project management fields of construction, aerospace, government and utilities , but also pharmaceuticals, information systems, finance/banking, telecommunications, product development (for many industries such as food, machinery, electronic, wood, and plastics), automotive, insurance and real-estate.

Fortune magazine recently labeled project management as the #1 career of the decade. In the same article, they wrote that with the delayering or downsizing of organizations, project management is replacing the middle manager.

I would like to ask those of you who are in the room to stand up if you carry the title of project manager or are directly involved with the field of project management. (Nearly everyone in the room stands.)

Now, I'd like to ask those who have a university degree in project management to remain standing while the others sit down. (The majority of those present sit down.)

As you can see, project management education is not taking place in the university for most of us. This means that our associations and organizations are carrying the load for development of the profession in terms of standards, education, training, and certification.

Global corporations are a significant driving force behind the growth of PMI. Multinational corporations are rapidly internalizing the standards and processes promoted by PMI. Companies such as AT&T, Siemens Corp., Asea Brown Boveri, AT&T GIS ,and so on, have implemented or are implementing formal project management processes. Many of these companies are integrating PMI's certification process into their career progression paths for project management professionals.

We have tremendous opportunities ahead. The leading project management software company estimates that the potential market share in the U.S. alone at over 10 million; this means, that in terms of membership in PMI, we have only begun to scratch the surface.

The many national and international associations represented here today are doing a tremendous job of serving our constituents. But we will be able to tremendously increase our effectiveness here today by modeling proven business techniques, such as working together, building strategic alliances, optimizing the synergy that exists among our organizations, and developing win-win solutions.

Just to address a couple of basic project management tenets:
- We have the authority to develop the project management profession.
- We have the accountability to build the project management profession.
- We have the responsibility to build the project management profession and to reach the millions of project management professionals that we represent around the world.

These are the reasons we are together today at this forum. Thank you for being a part of it.

Kent Crawford, PMP, formerly the senior manager for project management systems at The Analytic Sciences Corporation (TASC), is now president of Project Management Solutions, Inc. At TASC, he managed systems engineering work for a variety of customers including: Ameritech, Warner-Lambert, Procter & Gamble, Siemens, General Motors General Electric, the U.S. Department of Energy, the U.S. Air Force, and the U.S. Navy. Prior to joining TASC, he was Manager of Planning and Control for Monsanto Company. He is Chair of the Board of the Project Management Institute (PMI). As chair, Kent negotiated key alliances with the U.S. Department of Energy, the U.S. Corps of Engineers, the International Project Management Association (Europe), and the Australian Institute of Project Managers.

GLOBALIZATION OF PROJECT MANAGEMENT

Klaus Pannenbäcker
International Project Management Association (IPMA)

WE HAD TO change the name [of our organization] from INTERNET to avoid confusion [and] I want to highlight especially our new name, International Project Management Association.

First, let me say that I am really proud that my son, Olaf, is following me, and this gives me an occasion to ask you to think about your successors [in the project management profession].

In the past, IPMA put more emphasis on project management. Now we are dealing with projects in general and management of course, too. This [Global Forum] is a good chance for us to think about how we have to continue. IPMA [consists of] more than 25 countries and we now have round about 11,000 members. Really a big increase, and it's now time to come together with PMI, with AIPM, with other national associations, and to think about globalization. Otherwise, our partnership is too late if we are too "great."

IPMA is two years older, I believe, than PMI. It began when two friends, the French one and the German one, [sat] together in Paris and, after one or two bottles of champagne, as I was told, they decided we had to think about something like an international association for project management.

[One of my slides] will show you how many international conferences we have had in the past and where they were and [how they each focused on a] different competency. You see, the basic competencies of project management form the [project management] understanding itself. …Over the years, we see a trend of the key issues in our conferences going more towards the social competencies. The next conference in Paris in June 1996 is "Balancing Team and Task;" and two years later we will be in Ljubljana in Slovenia.

Where is Ljubljana? Ljubljana is the capital town of a very small country with 4 million inhabitants: Slovenia. Why should we elect Slovenia and Ljubljana for the next conference? Because I do hope that in three years' time these senseless wars in the Balkans will be finished, and then we have to revitalize a complete region. This will give an example of how to quickly revitalize damaged countries all over the world…

Okay, let me come back to my subject. Knowledge plus experience equals competence: it's a very simple equation. Knowledge requires education and training, plus practical work for the experience: this could be the basis for project manager certification. A qualification without the final certification makes no sense; everybody needs this for his or her personal career.

Of course, education and training must be based on something—the PMBOK standards, APM standards, European standards, etc. The practical work is based on my first

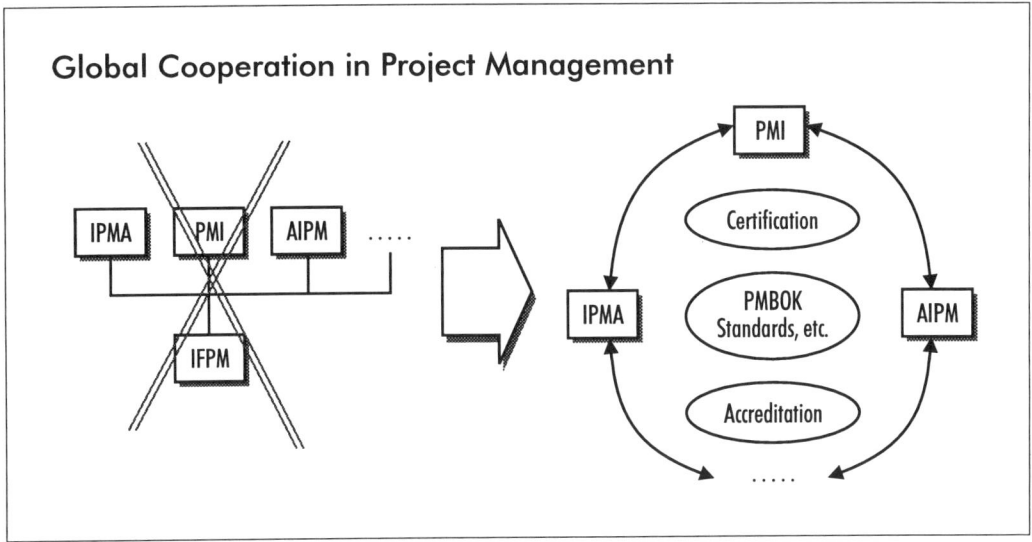

project, my second and [so on]; the projects I manage in my professional life. But the experience also comes by participating in symposiums, conferences, and expert seminars, in forums, and so on.

On the other hand, project management certification can also be based on a self-assessment principle, or on a work study or on an interview from your employer—whatever. But this certification, this high qualification must be accredited.

Let me continue with some other remarks. We have found out that not only individuals have to be educated and trained and finally qualified and certified, but we also have to think about how to train and qualify and certify the trainers to teach us. They have a specific career. And more and more in our countries [of IPMA] there is a need or demand from companies asking us "Can you improve the service of PM? Or our systems of controlling? Or our tools?" We have to think about our associations having the power, the accreditation, to improve those products. And for this, we have to put together a complete system of certification, and finally we need to accept it.

Accreditation: Two remarks. In Europe today we have a very hard problem in finding the right bodies of accreditation. And in addition, we have ... a lot of standards which even today we still don't completely understand if they are agreeing or disagreeing with each other. As an example, there are [various] standards existing for personal qualification, for product qualification, for PM software systems...

We have to concentrate ourselves on our internal products. I like to say that the PMBOK in itself can't be sold outside for real projects, it's only for the PM understanding. We have to concentrate on a qualification program, certification program, accreditation program.

Just last night I had a long conversation with Peter Morris (of APM). He said there is some confusion about the words we use; for example, in English, your certification would be my qualification. So we must deal with the language differences.

Let me add a story about what happened to me in 1990 when I gave a speech in Moscow that was translated from German into Russian. Afterwards, the big directors came up to me and said, "My dear *tovarisch*, all what you said, we have been doing since Lenin!"

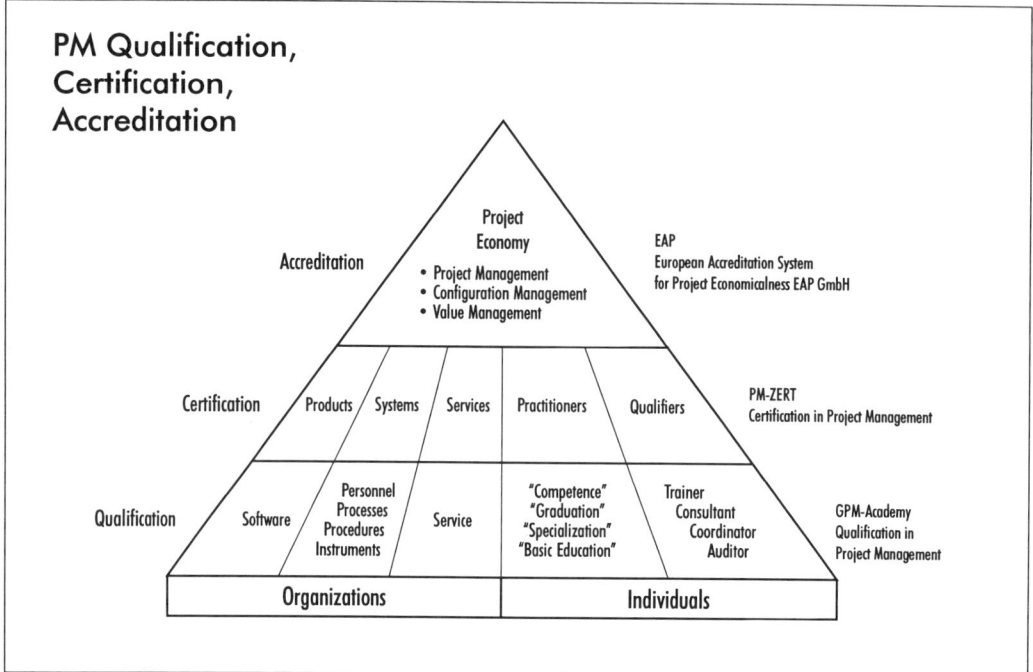

And I thought, "My goodness! This is not my best day!" and started to try to explain what I meant, but a friend stopped me and told me that the problem was the interpreter. He was using old words from the old times for new ideas. "You never missed," my friend told me, "but the interpreter gave the wrong impression to the audience." So, a common PM language is important.

We discussed all this in some meetings in Vancouver and in Sydney, how to come together. At a meeting in Sydney, we created the name International Federation of Project Management. Federation expresses the idea that everybody will stay in his own area and later on, we will sit together and discuss our products.

Let's start with a round table—like these we have here today—a round table is a specific method of how to come together, which we have used this past five years in talks between East Germany and West Germany, so that no one is at the head, no one is king or duke, with the others below him. On this round table, we want to hear from experts on how to deal with our four major products, which are the PMBOK, qualification, certification, and accreditation—accreditation, I have to highlight, must be on a very international basis. It makes no sense to have a German accreditation for German project managers, and then the Dutch, Norwegian, French, and Americans will say, "Well, Germany may accreditate this person but not here." So we must very much concentrate on an international system.

I see the need for a globalization of project management, for the unification of the PMBOK standards and so on for the certification and finally accreditation processes. But I want to highlight that the many national groups must stay in our organizations, in our associations, in our institutes and that education and training materials are mainly produced by the [unique] cultural districts. Of course we can learn from each other, but our

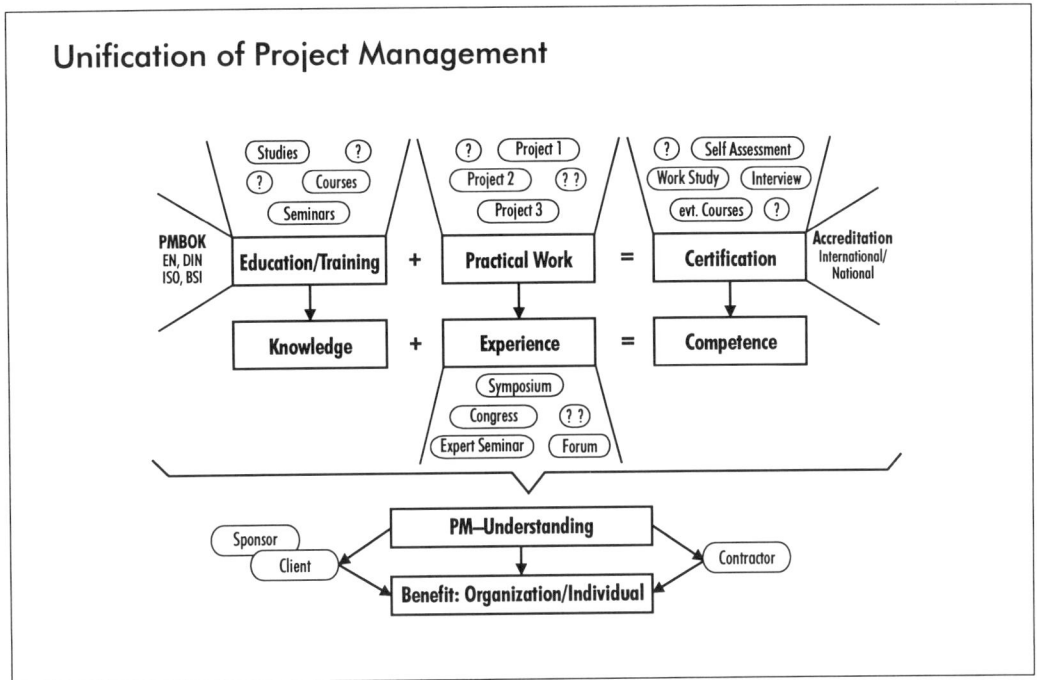

organizational products are really an expression of each national culture.

Finally, I want to give just one example of our internationality here at these round tables: I'd like to say Thanks … Danke … Merci … Gracias …(and Mr. Pannenbäcker continued, saying 'thank you" in all the languages represented at the Forum.)

Klaus Pannenbäcker is managing director and owner of Gesellschaft for Ablauforganisation and Informationsverarbeitung GABO mbH, a technical organizational consulting firm for industrial engineering and training in project management techniques. He was project manager of a German Project Management (PM) Body of Knowledge, the basis of a PM education with the official German certification PM Fachmann. He is also initiator of the IPMA Certification Programme. Since 1994 he is President of the International Project Management Association (IPMA), based in Europe, with 25 national Associations in West and East Europe as well as in some Asian countries.

THE GLOBAL PROJECT MANAGEMENT BODY OF KNOWLEDGE AND STANDARDS

Alan Stretton
Australian Institute of Project Management (AIPM)

I WILL BE brief because there is just one point I would like to make in relation to the development of a Global Body of Knowledge. For the past year, we have been conducting what I regard as a pilot program and we have developed a draft body of knowledge. When I say we, there are five people involved: myself from Australia, Bill Duncan from the USA, Richard Pharro from the U.K., Sebastian Dworatschek from Germany and Hiro Tanaka from Japan.

Now, we have only been able to have one meeting in that time—which we all had to contribute our own money to get to, incidentally! It's that sort of effort. And we have a draft model, with some supporting material, but it's fair to say that none of us regard that as being anything near approaching the last word. It's just the first step on a long, long route, I believe, to getting an acceptable core framework for a body of knowledge, one which everybody can subscribe to and be comfortable with, and can use and develop in their own cultural and business contexts, so that it really works for them.

Now to give you some idea of the situation: Those of you who have read through, or who will read through, the country reports that David Pells has provided, will see a huge variation in what people believe should be in the core PMBOK.

Further, for those of you who are not aware of it, there was a special issue in April of this year (1995) of the *International Journal of Project Management*, which was solely devoted to the Project Management Body of Knowledge. Once again, additional and wide-ranging differences of opinion as to what should be in there were expressed.

So my message, broadly, is this: Do not underestimate the magnitude of the task of developing a core body of knowledge that can be accepted universally. In particular, do not underestimate the amount of effort required, resources that are required, or commitment required from the organizations represented here. And that commitment includes very much a monetary commitment.

Believe me! Nothing that's worthwhile doing is easy. So I'm looking forward to being a co-facilitator in this afternoon's session on the Global Body of Knowledge. Thank you.

Alan Stretton has degrees from the University of Tasmania (B.E.) and the University of Oxford (M.A.). His first 38 years of experience were in the building and construction industries in Australia, the U.S. and New Zealand, including project management of construction, R&D, and organizational change projects. He then joined the University of Technology, Sydney (UTS), where he initiated a Master of Project Management course, now in its eighth year. He is immediate past-Chairman/Director of the Standards Committee of the Project Management Institute, and has held the corresponding position with the Australian Institute of Project Management (AIPM). In his current position as adjunct professor at UTS, his primary interests are in structured approaches to project management and supporting the development of a common structure that is globally applicable and accepted.

PROJECT MANAGEMENT STANDARDS IN JAPAN AND ENAA COOPERATION WITH ASIAN COUNTRIES

Hiroshi Tanaka
JGC Corp./ENAA

I REPRESENT ENAA where I am Vice Chair of the ENAA Project Management Committee. ENAA is a non-profit organization formed by Japanese EC companies based on corporate membership. I would first like to thank PMI for this excellent opportunity to give a speech on global project management issues, representing project management professionals in Asia.

Reflecting the trends in the Japanese project management circle, we have four objectives to pursue through this PM global networking:

First, we would like to make our best efforts to enhance the social and industrial status of project managers who are so hardworking, high-performing and innovative, yet who are less known in society than they should be: for this, we would like to join forces with our project management peers from other parts of the world.

Second, we would like to expand the application areas of project management to as many industry sectors and public services in Japan as possible from the current limited applications, mainly in engineering and construction. We hope that project management processes will not remain the monopoly of the construction industry and will prove to be highly effective tools for productivity enhancement for the overall Japanese industry. We would like to find out about as many cases as possible elsewhere in the world in which project management potentials have been exploited in non-construction fields.

Third, we would like to make available to Japanese project management professionals the international project management standards that have been published by PMI and those that will be produced through the international networking that we are seeing today.

We are very happy with the revised PMBOK and the Core Framework for Project Management Knowledge being developed by representatives of PMI, IPMA, APM, AIPM and ENAA.

The fourth objective would be to discuss the possibility of forming global industry-specific interest groups. The companies enrolled with ENAA are all engaged in the engineering and construction business.

In addition to this overall global project management forum, we would like to see industry branch forums to enable closer exchange of ideas aligned to specific interests.

The theme of PMI '95 is communication. My first experience in delivering messages on project management in Japan was back in 1981 during the INTERNET congress in Copenhagen. There I met Dr. John Adams of PMI for the first time and he encouraged me to keep on communicating with the rest of the project management world. From that time on, I started trying to follow his advice, coming to PMI annual meetings and communicating with my project management peers, both casually and through paper presentations, business meetings with PMI leaders and a U.S.-Japan cross-cultural project management seminar at Western Carolina University in Cullowhee, North Carolina, as well as through project management technology exchange meetings with U.S. organizations related to project management. Many such communications were carried out while I was on ENAA's project management delegation to North America. I presume that I have been offered this opportunity to talk to you because of this background.

The original title of the speech that was assigned to me was "Project Management Standards in Asia and the Pacific." However, I would like to modify it to read "Project Management Standards in Japan and ENAA Project Management Cooperation with Asian Countries."

Under this revised title, I would like to report on what standard project management knowledge documents we have at ENAA, the preparation of the Japanese language version of the PMBOK with which we are proceeding, and then what type of cooperation in project management training ENAA has extended to Asian countries.

To be exact, we have no standard for project management in Japan in any form equivalent to or similar to the Guide to Project Management Body of Knowledge of PMI. However, we do have this handbook of project operations and project management published in 1986 by the ENAA Project Management Committee. This book is in between a glossary of project management terms and a handbook.

This handbook contains 560 pages and consists of six parts and 23 chapters.
- Part 1 is an introduction to Context of Project Operations and Framework of Project Management.
- Part 2 deals with the Management of Pre-contract Project Work such as Proposals, Bidding, and Contracting.
- Part 3 discusses Project Organization and Human Resources Management and Project Professional Development.
- Part 4 is the core and provides Project Management Processes, covering: Project Planning, Cost Estimating, Project Schedule Planning and Control, Cost Management, Quality Management and Manpower Management.
- The reference also covers, in Part 5, the Management of Line Work Execution of: Engineering Design, Purchasing, Logistics, Construction and Commissioning.
- Part 6 covers Project Support and Administration Services, including: Project Management, Information System (PMI's), Site Administration, Accounting and Taxation, Finance, Foreign Exchange, and Insurance and Bonds.

Although the handbook is written in Japanese, the contents are not typically Japanese but are based on common practices in the worldwide engineering and construction industry as the most active participants in ENAA activities are companies in this business.

Management Part I, II and III, published in 1981, 1982 and 1983; Guide to Human Resources Management, published in 1981; Guide to Project Cost Management, published in 1983; Guide to Schedule Planning and Control in 1984; Cost Engineering in the '90s, published in 1992; and Project Management Information Systems Guide, in 1993.

These reports are deliverables of research task forces formed by the ENAA PM Committee and provide the basic practices and techniques as well as describe the context in which these project management processes are applied. These reports are disseminated to ENAA member companies. And, project management basic training courses are held by ENAA with industry project management professionals as instructors twice a year along more or less these lines.

The characteristics of these documents are such that engineering and construction projects are considered as almost the sole application area and that project control techniques for relatively large projects are highlighted.

Now, our lessons learned are that, as Dr. Peter Morris mentioned in his speech, these industry-specific knowledge documents make sense, however, project management as discipline applicable to all business fields is weakened. Then, what are we doing?

Now, ENAA's project management committee is proceeding with the development of the Japanese language version of the revised PMBOK of PMI through a task force headed by myself. The Task Force has completed its translation based on the PMBOK exposure draft, and since the formal updated PMBOK will soon be released, we will make adjustments in the Japanese version documents; then the Task Force will issue an exposure draft to about ten senior members of the committee for comments. If we apply the performance index given in Chapter 7, Cost Management of PMBOK, I think we will be able to issue the Japanese version sometime in February next year, pending PMI permission for publication.

The Japanese version PMBOK is being awaited eagerly by project people at Japanese companies affiliated with ENAA for the following reasons:

First of all, it is written in Japanese and relieves the headaches of Japanese engineers who have limited exposure to the international project arena and do not find it fun to read English.

The PMBOK is thorough, comprehensive and consistent, yet concise and easy to read. It's a benchmark collection of project management processes and, thus, is a good entry framework book for project management professionals.

By way of the PMBOK, project management professionals, regardless of experience level, have a common lexicon concerning project management.

Amid the ever-increasing internationalization of project operations of Japanese companies, by familiarizing yourself with the PMBOK, you can keep abreast with international PM standards, as opposed to local ones which have limitations in applicability in the other parts of the world.

The PMBOK does not carry the smell—or should I say fragrance because we live on that—of oil, petrochemicals and concrete, but can apply to projects in whatever application areas. There are emerging needs for project management methods and practices in Japanese industry branches other than engineering and construction: say the manufacturing and information services industries among others. They welcome the new PMBOK as a project management standard that offers wide applicability. And this need coincides with the objective of the ENAA project management committee, which advocates selling project management grown in engineering and construction to as many industries as possible.

So much for our project management standards in Japan. At this time, I would like to report on ENAA's project management training initiatives in collaboration with Asian countries.

International cooperation is one of ENAA's objectives. As part of our international cooperation programs, ENAA has, to date, organized seven project management seminars in five host countries since 1985.

The countries which have hosted ENAA PM seminars are Indonesia, Thailand, Vietnam, Kazakhstan and China. These seminars are two- to five-day courses and include such subjects as Project Management Framework, Planning and Schedule Management, Cost Management, Procurement Management, and Quality Management/Quality Assurance. The courses offer both lectures and mini workshops which are taught by Japanese international contractor companies' officers and firstline project directors/managers or project control managers.

The host organizations have been government agencies of those countries. If we look at the motives of hosting organizations in requesting ENAA project management seminars, they uniformly stress their desire to learn project management of lump sum turnkey projects, to which the Japanese contractors are extensively exposed. In this sense, the audience has expected that as practical planning and control techniques as possible be included in the seminar.

We at ENAA feel that managing lump sum engineering and construction projects is the topic we can talk over.

This concludes my report on project management professional development in Japan. Thank you once again for this opportunity to present ENAA's activities.

Hiroshi (Hiro) Tanaka is Deputy General Manager of Operations Administration and Services at JGC Corporation, a leading Japanese engineering and construction company. He holds a bachelor degree in political science from Keio University. In his current position, he is responsible for JGC's overall administration of project operations, project management technology, corporate quality assurance, quality control, construction safety, vendor qualification/registration and experience in the engineering and construction industry serving mainly the oil and gas and chemicals industry. He is a twelve-year PMI member, Vice Chair of the Project Management Committee of the Engineering Advancement Association of Japan (ENAA), which is Japan's sole association promoting project management, and a member of IPMA. He has served as the focal point for bridging ENAA and PMI with his five-time attendance at PMI annual meetings and other types of contacts.

GLOBAL PROJECT MANAGEMENT CERTIFICATION

Brian Kooyman
Australian Institute of Project Management (AIPM)

I CONSIDER MYSELF fortunate to have attended initial Global Project Management meetings in Vancouver (October 1994), Philadelphia (December 1994), and Sydney (April 1995). I also welcome the opportunity to speak at this Global Forum in New Orleans and wish the future of such a forum every success.

However, as identified at meetings previous to this forum, it is important to recognize the substantial enormity of the tasks ahead of this group. To achieve any modicum of success will require significant manpower, and financial resources that will thoroughly test every participant's commitment to the process.

At the initial meetings of Philadelphia and Sydney, many good principles were developed and these should not be simply discarded, particularly for personal or territorial reasons.

On the positive side it is good to note that there are a number of these initial developments that remain on this Global Forum agenda, importantly, the recognition of the following points:

1. The problem of terminology between not only culturally different associations, but even between English-speaking associations
2. The need to continue the development of a global core body of knowledge
3. The need and desire for recognition of accreditation and certification.

These last two items are, in my mind, fundamental as the foundation stones or building blocks for any global cooperation.

I have been asked to talk about certification, however, I would stress that I do not offer myself as an expert in this area (there are others better qualified), but I will endeavor to provide a personal perspective and the experience of the Australian environment.

For the meetings in Philadelphia and Sydney, the reason four associations (PMI, IPMA, AIPM, and APM) were involved is because they were seen as having already progressed, or were substantially progressed, down the path of certification.

Within these certification processes, two distinct philosophical approaches were identified with regard to recognition of those working professionally within project management: One is testing of project management people primarily by an examination process, i.e. the PMP process, and all credit to PMI for having established this first milestone for project management. The second philosophy is by competency assessment, or a process to assess the ability of a person to apply project management knowledge in the workplace.

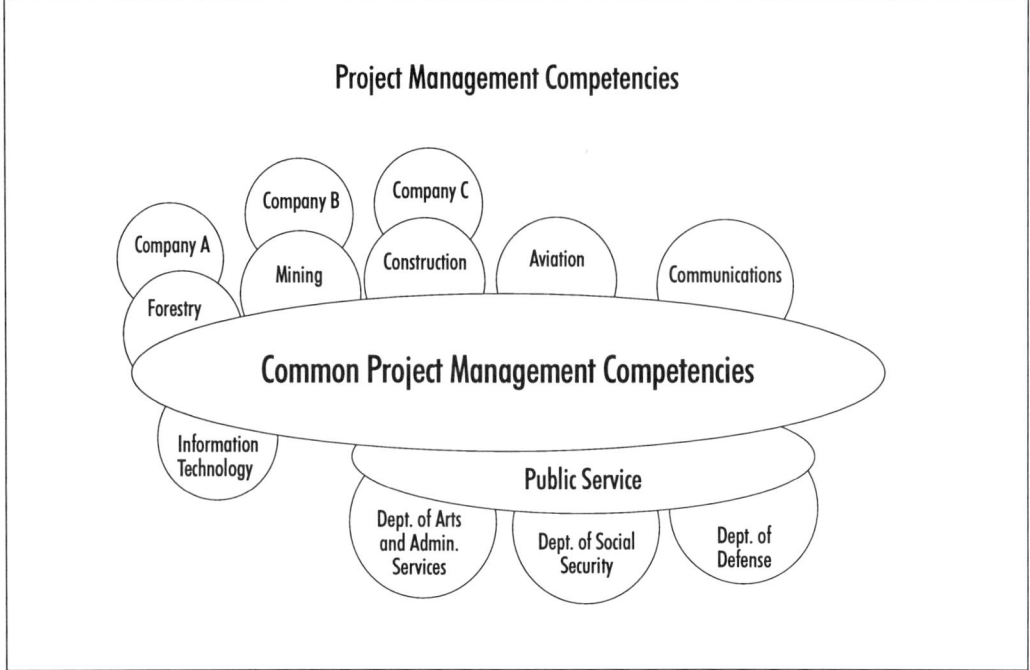

This cannot be tested by an examination-dominated process, it must find a methodology to review application in the workplace.

This second philosophy is the driving force behind the Australian experience, and I have been advised that a similar motivation is fueling the United Kingdom (APM's) approach. Substantial preparatory work has now been done by both organizations (AIPM and APM) and the resultant processes are now moving forward.

At this stage, I believe it is important to conclude that my opinion is the two philosophies are not opposed, rather the second is a natural evolution of the first.

I believe project management should face this evolutionary process if we intend avoiding becoming "old people's clubs," and more preferably become proactive in working with industries to understand their needs and anticipate changing needs. To explain this, I would refer to the AIPM's experience where the Australian government would not recognize any award by an examination-dominated process.

Government in Australia is committed to workplace reform and restructuring. Productivity gains must be quantified and thus any assessment based on competency.

Competency is defined as:
1. Knowledge—may be tested by examination
2. Skill—may be evaluated by experience
3. Attribute or Attitude—may be evaluated by interview, but must assess the application of knowledge and skill.

Through the AIPM (as facilitator) and the bringing together of an "industries reference group," Australia has now developed the final review draft of the national competency standards for Australian project management.

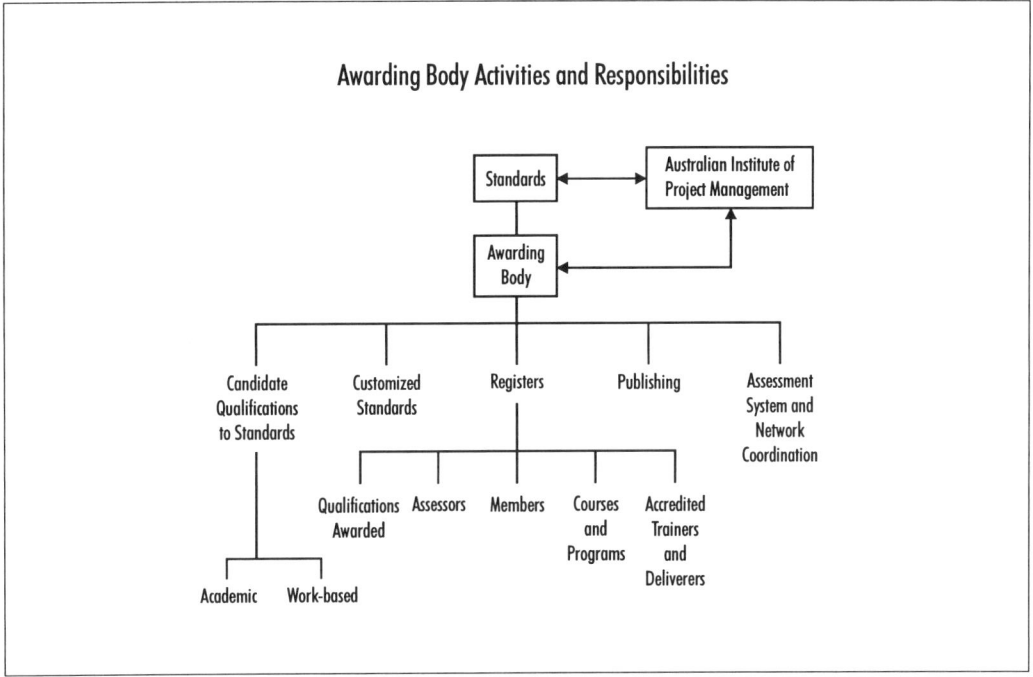

As indicated on the first diagram, these are generic standards from which each industry will develop industry specific standards, and organizations can develop corporate specific standards. However, the foundation stone is the generic competency standards.

AIPM's role will be as guardian and responsible for continued development of the competency standards, and we are now looking at the process where people can either be assessed through an AIPM process (i.e. most likely exam, experience/project report and by interview), or by workplace assessment. Both methods must be available.

The potential organizational diagram for this is indicated on the second diagram.

An important factor within the Australian competency standards is their relationship of criteria underpinning a competence to levels within a project management team.

As indicated in the third diagram, there is more than a project manager comprising a project team, and associations must respond to the needs of all those that make up a project team.

The Australian competency standards through their performance relationship to identified project management levels, attempts to address this concept.

Within the Australian framework, a project management professional starts at Level 4, a professional project manager starts at Level 6.

I would suggest that this concept provides a possible bridge between the existing PMP assessment and the competency assessment.

Perhaps, more importantly, this concept could provide a framework for "calibration" of existing and virtually completed certification standards between associations or institutes.

Experience has and is showing us that "national" and "cultural" differences must be

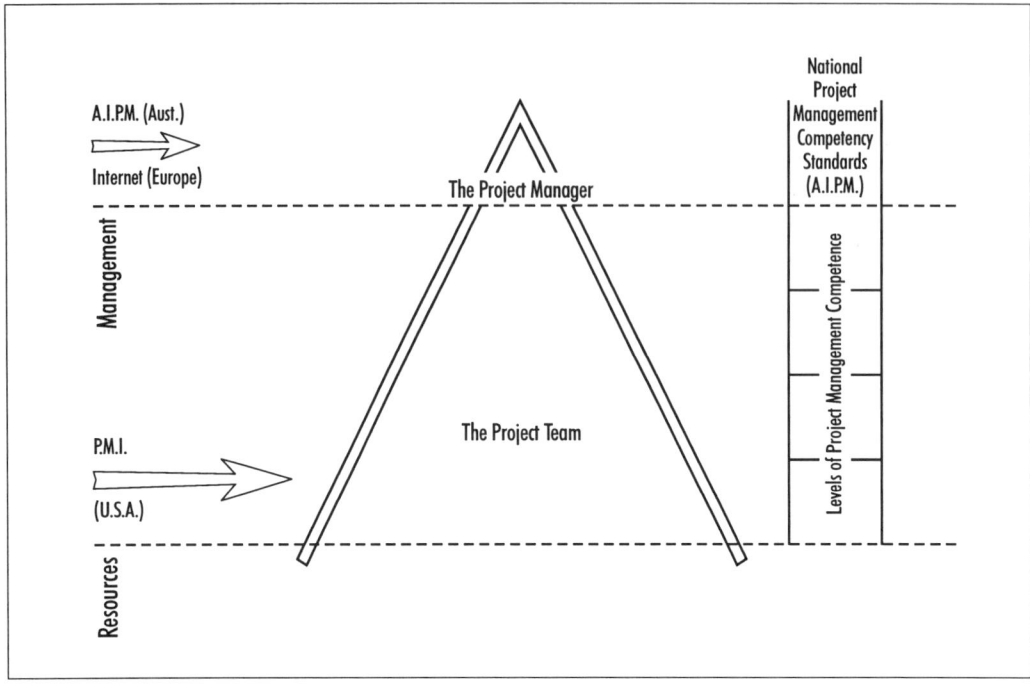

maintained—this will prove an interesting challenge for global project management, as we will need to find the means of calibrating and connecting a global framework for certification.

Ladies and gentlemen, if we can achieve this global framework the rewards are substantial. We will:
- Develop project management as a profession that responds to industry needs and change.
- Develop transportable certification around the world that is a benefit to "all" our members, and to multi-national organizations.
- Set standards that are truly international and that respond to world bank, Asian Development Bank and other international industry needs.
- Improve communication, standards of terminology and the body of knowledge.
- Do what no other profession has done!

The challenge is ours, and it is here now!

Brian R. Kooyman, A.R.A.I.A., M.A.I.P.M., is managing director of Tracey, Brunstrom & Hammond Pty Ltd. and immediate past national president of the Australian Institute of Project Management (A.I.P.M.). During the 20 years as an architect and project manager, He has worked on numerous large projects in Australia, including the Sydney Harbour Casino, the Darling Harbour Redevelopment Project and The Queen Elizabeth Medical Centre. He has been involved in the Australian Institute of Project Management for over eight years as New South Wales Chapter President, National President (1993–1995), and as Chairman of the Professional Affairs Committee (1990–1993).

PROJECT MANAGEMENT IN LATIN AMERICA

Paul Dinsmore, PMP
Dinsmore and Associates, Rio de Janiero, Brazil

LATIN AMERICA, WHICH stretches from the Rio Grande in Texas to Tierra Del Fuego at the tip of South America, was in the spotlight during the PMI 1995 Global Forum in New Orleans, which took place concurrently with U.S. First Lady Hillary Clinton's visit to four Latin American countries. There are other reasons for the world to focus on this sometimes overlooked part of the global economy:

- For the last four years, the Latin American economy has grown at 3.5 percent, about 50 percent more than the world average, which was 2.4 percent. In 1994, Peru alone grew 13 percent.
- According to the Interamerican Development Bank, Latin America has gone from one of the most protected economies in the world to one of the most open.
- Latin America covers about one sixth of the world's area.
- The population is expected to reach 1.5 billion by year 2000.
- In Denver 1995, the NAFTA, Mercosul, Andean Pact and Central American communities signed an agreement to form the FTAA (Free Trade Area of the Americas) by the year 2005, which will encompass 850 million consumers.

All of this points to continued economic growth (predicted at 3.7 percent per year for the remainder of the decade). This naturally calls for project management expertise for upcoming capital projects. This includes both "hard" project management for engineering and construction projects as well as "soft" project management for organizational change projects. Here are some of the areas in expansion:

- Pulp and paper: Riding high on strong profits and investing towards the future.
- Oil and gas: Gas pipelines are underway and oil exploration is on the increase. In Argentina YPF was privatized in 1993. This trend extends to other Latin American oil companies as well.
- Telecommunications: Privatization is also a strong trend. Over the next five years, over $80 billion is expected to be invested in Latin American telecommunications.

There is no association for project management in Latin America. PMI has about 30 members who reside in Latin America.

The one organization that congregates many major consulting companies that offer project management services is called FEPAC—Federation Panamericana De Consulotores (Pan-American Federation of Consultants). Since capital is scarce, these consulting companies are now obliged to help search for project financing so they can propose package deals.

FEPAC, using interamerican bank financing, has coordinated a series of project management seminars throughout Latin America for its member associations.

Opportunity abounds in Latin America, although the challenges are great. There is great reason for the rest of the world, and certainly the project management community, to continue to focus on Latin America.

Paul Dinsmore, PMP, joined the Project Management Institute in 1977 and is a PMI Fellow. He has made notable contributions to both the theory and practice of project management. His contributions to PMI include articles in PM Network, Seminar/Symposia papers, and PMI books. He has also participated in INTERNET activities and has been an international contributor in bringing PMI and INTERNET closer in their complementary roles. Dinsmore has published several management books in both English and Portuguese, including The AMA Handbook of Project Management and Human Factors in Project Management, as well as more than 60 articles and papers. He is the managing director of Dinsmore Associates, with offices in Dallas, Texas, USA and Rio de Janeiro and San Paulo, Brazil. He has performed consulting work in North and South America, Africa, and Europe.

PROJECT MANAGEMENT IN EMERGING ECONOMIES

Vladimir I. Voropajev
SOVNET (Russia)

Project management, as understood in the '70s–'90s has been based on the experience of technically developed countries with relatively stable economic conditions such as the United Kingdom, Germany, Holland, the United States, Canada, Australia, and Japan.

But at the present time, project managers from developing and transitional economy countries are actively joining the "world of project management." The movement for project management professional development now bears a global character. Two tendencies can be marked:

- A growing number of firms and companies from developing countries are involved in international economic activity, including cooperation with developed countries.
- A growing number of investors and other project participants from developed countries are engaged in projects and programs implemented in developing countries.

These processes show that both the world economy and the whole world community are becoming increasingly integrated. Obviously, this process requires the development of a common language for business communication and creation of a global professional business culture for joint creative activity. Modern project management can and, in my opinion, must be such a universal tool.

Developing countries can choose among several methods of project management development and application. They can take the experience of PMI in North America as a basis; take the experience of Europe as a basis (IPMA); choose orientation to neighboring or culturally similar countries; develop their own approach based on home experience, achievements, traditions and cultures; or take the most advanced experience and knowledge of the world and develop a national project management based on international cooperation, unification and globalization—while saving national traditions and culture.

I believe this last way is much preferable, more efficient and practical for developing countries, as it allows them to overcome dragging behind the world level and avoid possible problems and mistakes.

The special features of the project environment in developing countries are mainly caused by the dynamics of development. The deepest large-scale and rapid changes have occurred since the early '90s in Russia, former USSR republics and countries of Eastern Europe. Therefore my statements are based on Russian data and experience, because they reflect the general tendencies of modern world development and can be applied, to a certain extent, to all developing countries.

The Global Status of the Project Management Profession

I agree with Dr. Martin Barnes, who, in his article "The Future for Project Management" (International Journal of Project Management August, 1993), said that nowadays all countries are developing; their division into developed and developing is merely conditional and depends on the achieved level of development, intensity of development, and the stability of the social and economic environment.

Nevertheless, there are three levels of development:
- Developed—slow evolutionary development in stable social and economic environment (Great Britain, USA, Japan and so on).
- Developing—rapid evolutionary development in relatively unstable social and economic environment (China, India, Indonesia and so on).
- Transitional—very rapid development with changes of revolutionary type in unstable and economic environment (former USSR, Eastern Europe countries and so on).

So, in a sense, we all live in developing and changing countries, and we should assist in managing such changes, trying to use them for the good of our countries and the whole of mankind. Change itself forms the "nutrient medium" for the development of project management and can serve as the basis for project management global unification.

Taking the former USSR as an example, we can consider the following important characteristics of project management development. Project-oriented activity in Russia during this period is characterized by:
- A rapid change in the structure of projects and an increase in the number of projects in non-traditional spheres
- A decrease of the number of long-term programs and mega-projects in connection with risk increase and reduced share of centralized investments
- A change in the traditional spheres of project activity application and their re-orientation to branches with short payback periods and to owners (customers) and users
- A change in investment policy, structure and sources of investments including reducing investments to the sphere of production from 70 percent to 50 percent and increase of investments to non-production sphere (up to 50 percent).

Some major features of the changing of social and economic systems in Russia are:
- Sharply changing property relations
- Political and economic instability
- Sharp differentiation and decrease of living conditions with simultaneous decrease of social and legal guarantees for the population
- High tax rates
- Crisis of economy and production
- Lack of legal regulation, especially in the sphere of investment
- Non-coordinated activity between federal power structures and subjects of federation
- Underdeveloped market infrastructure
- High degree of criminal activity.

From a project management point of view, all these processes show a high level of project environment changes as well as financial and other risks, a great demand for investments and relatively cheap market of labor and services.

How do the characteristics of a transitional economy influence project activity and project management? Political and economic change that occurred in Russia caused changes both in project activities and in style and methods of management. Changes in the project context included:

- The structure, type, scale and duration of projects and programs as well as the spheres of their application
- The structure of project organizational participants, their mutual relations, property relation within the project, functions, motivation system, sanctions, etc
- Organizational forms and structures of project-oriented activity
- Close and distant project environment
- The structure of expenses during the project life-cycle.

These changes, in their turn, caused considerable difference in such project management characteristics as:

- Project purposes, scope, conditions, limits and requirements
- Systems of value and ethical norms, criteria of project analysis efficiency and project results estimation
- Integrative in project management: concept and project development, planning, control, system of documentation and reporting
- The structure, role and methods of realization of project management functions.

In the West, project management was brought to life by the market economy in order to increase the efficiency of project realization. However, even though modern project management is necessary it is not allowed to become a sphere of professional activity in a centralized economy. For example, before the reforms in Russia started in 1990, project management was not applied or practiced to its fullest extent.

In a transitional period, when the risk and level of changes in project environment are very high, the necessity for object project management necessity is highest, also. Under free-market conditions the need for project management remains very high, although lower than in transitional periods. This is because a stable social and economic environment causes reduced risk.

As a transitional economy grows towards becoming a market economy, the need for all project management functions increases. The functions most sensitive to change are risk, procurement, contracts, scope, configuration, communications and information, which reach the maximum end of necessity transitional period. The functions less exposed to these factors—quality, time, cost, human resources—increase more gradually as they approach the market economy.

From my research, it is possible to make some general conclusions concerning project management in different social and economic conditions.

- Social and economic environments of all types are subject to change and, therefore, they can be considered as developing.
- Transitional economies, due to frequency and intensity of changes, can be considered from a project management point of view, as the most common case of social and economic project environment.

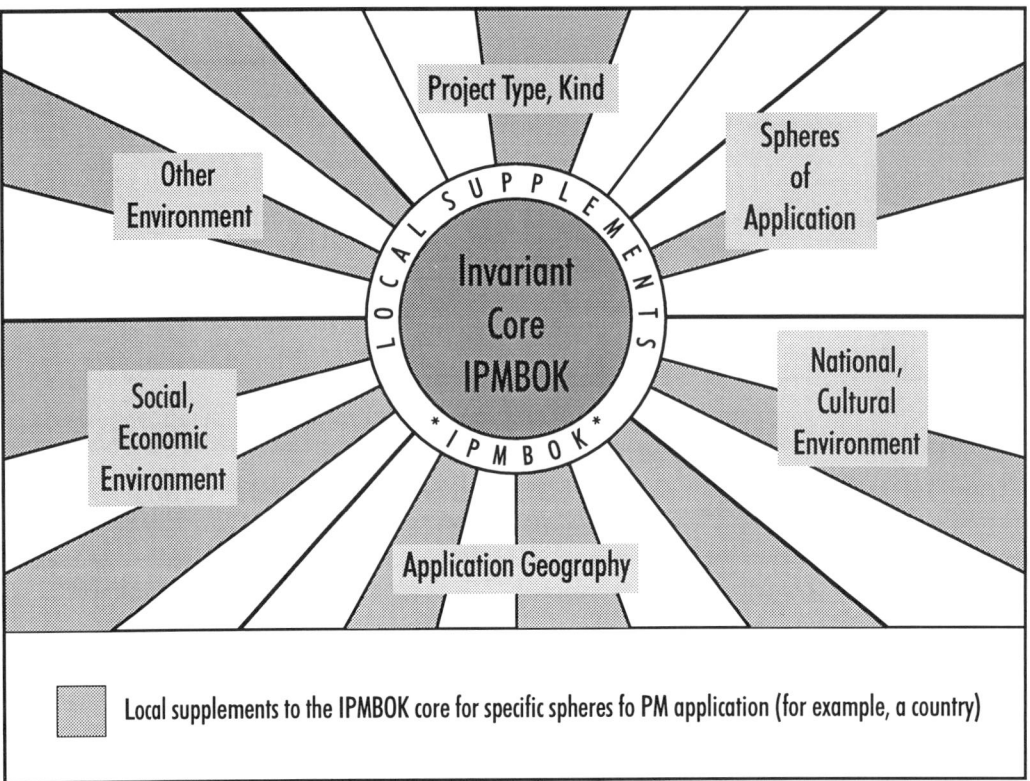

- All types of economies need project management applications but economies in transition from centralized economy to market one, the necessity for project management methods and tools application, considerably grows.
- The scientific basis, of the project management PMBOK structure and core, including the context of project management functions, is valid in spite of the difference between the economies themselves.
- Difference in project management under different social and economic environments is not principle-centered and does not affect the basis of project management. As a rule, any differences relate to the types of projects implemented, specific features of spheres of their application, the natural environment, or methods of project management practical use. All these differences would be considered within the frames of local supplements to the PMBOK core and in special guides and recommendations on project management application.
- In the transition to a market economy, the probability of changes in a project and its environment, as well as risks, increase sharply. This tendency is also peculiar to the market economy. In this case, common for all economies, we can define project management as managing changes in changing "parent" organization under the influence of changing external environment. This circumstance requires introducing a new project management integrative function, "Change Management" which should cover traditional functions of Configuration Management and Overall

Change Control and have not only operative, reactive character, but also solve tasks of change forecasting and preventing. Change Management is connected with all aspects of the project itself, all project management functions and processes.

International Project Management Development

Further project management development in both developing and developed countries should be based on two closely connected approaches:

- Global development is international and covers components of project management professional activity invariant to project management practice and spheres of application.
- Local development is national or oriented to another specific sphere of application (for example, country, region, trans-national company, branch, etc.). In local project management development we should take into account political, social, economic, technological and other specific features of project management practice and spheres of application.

Such development must take place on three levels:

- Project management globalization means forming a global, common understanding and world-wide recognition for project management as:

  - A special sphere of professional activity spread world-wide and covering all possible spheres of project management application;

  - A separate, complex applied scientific discipline with its theory, methodology, spheres and practice of application;

  - A profession requiring special knowledge, skills and competence for successful project management.

- Project management unification is forming and developing unified project management components, elements, processes and procedures for all countries.

- Project management localization means forming and working out the various project management components and elements reflecting the specific features of different spheres of project management application, practical experience, and cultural factors.

Project Management Globalization

Project management globalization should solve the following problems:

- Forming and providing a global project management understanding and recognition as a sphere of special activity, scientific discipline and profession.
- Forming a scientific basis for project management including:

  - International project management language (terms, definitions, notions, glossary, thesaurus, dictionaries, etc.);

  - Developing basis of project management theory and methodology;

  - Developing project management international core and PMBOK invariant to the spheres of project management application and practice.

- Organization, support and coordination of global cooperation of project management organizations and specialists.

Project Management Unification

Project management unification should include:
- Developing as International Body of Knowledge (IPMBOK) invariant core and distant sectors with flexible structure reflecting specific features of spheres and conditions of project management application. The unified structure of IPMBOK will assist each country, industry and company in forming their own individual IPMBOK configurations.
- Common approach to education and personnel training of project managers at all levels.
- International program based on IPMBOK for preparing specialists.
- International concept, requirements, programs and procedures for certification and accreditation of project management specialists and organizations.

The steps in project management unification might be:
- Developing an international program and procedures for project management specialists knowledge qualification based on PMBOK and the PMP certification programs worked out by PMI and updated with materials for IPMA, AIPM, ISO and so on (first level of certification).
- Developing an international programs and procedures for certification of project managers, confirming their competence based on IPMBOK and IPMA certification programs, updated with materials from PMI and other international organizations (second level of certification).
- The same on the program of accreditation (see Sections 1, 2).
- Appropriate national certification programs can be developed based on Steps 1, 2, and 3.
- A system of international standards and normative bases, into practice through the international organizations.

Project Management Localization

Project management localization includes development of local supplements, adaptation of global and unified project management components and elements to specific conditions of the spheres of project management application and practice. Such supplements include:
- Adaptation of IPMBOK to specific conditions.
- Creating national project management language compatible with the international one.
- Creating national system of education, certification, qualification of specialists and accreditation of project management organizations.
- Development of special project management methods and tools, methodical recommendations and guides on project management application taking into consideration local conditions and requirements.
- Development of guiding and methodical project management materials within the frames of firm.

So, specific trends and a practical course of project management application in Russia should be defined in the process of localization, taking into consideration specific features of transitional economy and results of project management unification and globalization.

Principles of International Organization and Coordination of Work on Project Management Development

For realization of the international program of project management development, appropriate organizational forms, intellectual and financial support are necessary.

Organizational forms to support global project management complex development could take many forms. The most acceptable form is creating the International Federation of Project Management Association (IFPMA), which can unite all existing international, regional and national project management associations and organizations.

The main purposes of IFPMA could be:
- Global development of the project management profession and its promotion in new countries, regions and spheres of application
- Project management unification and standardization
- Development and realization of international program and projects on education, scientific research, qualification, certification of project managers and accreditation of project management organizations
- Holding project management forums
- Information and publishing activity and services for IFPMA members
- Organization and coordination of IFPMA members in project management development.

IFPMA should be managed by the elected for 2-3 years coordination group and should not have rigid vertical hierarchic structure of a bureaucratic type.

To create IFPMA it is necessary:
- To create an initiative group
- To develop the concept and draft Charter of IFPMA
- To obtain consent of international and national organizations to join IFPMA and come to agreement on constituent documents
- To hold the Constituent Conference.

Intellectual support of global project management development and unification should be performed by and under the aegis of IFPMA members.

For this purpose the following should be done:
- Forming temporary working commissions and groups from authorized experts for realization of IFPMA projects. The list of experts should be confirmed by IFPMA members.
- Periodical discussions on work results, projects and programs during IFPMA working meetings and forums
- Review and approving the final project management documents on IFPMA projects
- Presenting approved project management documents to competent international organizations.

Financial support of projects and programs on project management globalization, unification and localization should be performed by international foundations, international financial and crediting institutions, governments of countries concerned, national organizations and transnational companies.

The proposed approach to further project development in the world and each separate country allows to obtain the following profits:
- Acceleration of the process of integration of the world community and its social and economic development
- Providing further efficient development of project management all over the world
- Acceleration of project management knowledge and experience transfer to developing countries and their social and economic, scientific and technical progress
- Expanding the experience, achievements, national and cultural values of all countries in the field of project management
- Opening new spheres of project management application in our developing world.

Vladimir I. Voropajev, Ph.D., is a hydrotechnical engineer and a certified professor of management information systems. He has served as president of the Russian Project Management Association (SOVNET) since 1991 and is currently vice president for Developing and Transition Economy Countries of the International Project Management Association (IPMA). Professor Voropajev is one of the leading theoretical experts on project management in the former Soviet Union and has published many technical papers on project management topics. He has assisted the World Bank with development of a Project Management Training Program for Russia.

PROJECT MANAGEMENT SUPPORT OF ECONOMIC DEVELOPMENT

Robert Youker
World Bank (Retired)

PROJECTS ARE VERY important in economic development. They are the way a country adds to its productive capital. They are also a source of funds from the international community. Projects are both hard, like dams and schools, and soft like training farmers and developing new school curricula. Project management is obviously important in implementing projects and in meeting time, cost and performance objectives. In this brief presentation I am going to discuss seven conclusions and recommendations from my experience in working in more than thirty countries around the globe.

1. You must think about managing the entire project life cycle from pre-feasibility study to design and financing and not just the implementation or construction phase. Project Management Standards and Certification must expand their focus to include the earlier phases in the life cycle.

2. In developing countries, implementation is much more of a problem on soft projects like educational reform than hard projects like electric power plants. As Russ Archibald said at our first conference 28 years ago, "we must learn how to apply project management to knowledge workers as well as manual workers." Project Management Standards and Certification again need to expand their focus and include soft projects.

3. Implementation is a difficult issue for lending agencies like the World Bank and the regional banks because they are financing agencies and the borrower or operating agency is responsible for implementation. This means the consulting and training business is with the countries and not the banks.

4. A key implementation problem in most countries and agencies is the mismatch between strong traditional functional organizational structures and the needs of the project which cut across the functional departments. Organizational design entails a compromise between the long-term needs of the functional structure and the short-term needs of the project. Outside agencies like the World Bank should be cautious about recommending matrix structures like project implementation units without knowing the requirements for making a matrix work or the long-run implications of a temporary matrix structure. Project Management Standards and Certification should cover this issue.

5. Many problems of implementation in developing countries are not related to the internal issues of control as listed in the basic PMBOK but are in the environment external to the project such as the Ministry of Finance not releasing funds. The Standards and Certification efforts need to reflect this fact.

6. The communication problems in the field of project management are just as serious or more serious within countries as between countries. In China, for example, strong vertical ministries do not communicate well with each other for a variety of reasons. At a conference in Brazil I found that university professors were not in communication with the consulting profession. External agencies like PMI and IPMA can be mindful of this problem and try to foster internal communication.

7. There are excellent business opportunities in the global marketplace. The international lending agencies and the countries need help in appraising the implementation capacity of organizations and assistance in training and in setting up management systems for projects. The decision-making is in the countries and success will be based on making local contacts and adjusting to the local situation and culture including partnerships with local consultants.

In conclusion, let me say that the publications section of the Economic Development Institute of the World Bank has a complete set of training materials including readings, overheads, exercises and cases in English, Spanish, French, Arabic, Chinese and Russian languages. The materials are in the public domain and available for a nominal fee. The address of the World Bank is Washington, DC , USA, 20433.

Robert Youker is an independent consultant and trainer in project implementation operating from Bethesda, Maryland, USA. From 1988 to 1991 he was an Adjunct Professor of Project Management in the Engineering Management School of George Washington University. He has taught short courses for Harvard University, University of Wisconsin, Asian Development Bank, A.D. Little and the University of Bradford, England among others. His recent consultancy assignments include evaluating the Monitoring System for the island of St. Kitts for the Organization of American States and an evaluation of the project implementation process for the African Development Bank. From 1975 to 1987, he worked at the World Bank, first as a lecturer at the Economic Development Institute and later as a management specialist in the Institutional Development Division for Africa. He is a graduate of Colgate University and the Harvard Business School and took doctoral studies in Behavioral Science at George Washington University.

PART III

THE GROUP PROCESS

REPORTS FROM THE BREAKOUT SESSIONS

INTRODUCTION

David L. Pells, PMP
Global Forum Project Manager

Five afternoon breakout sessions were held for attendees to participate in discussions on key issues of common professional interest around the world. Although the large number of delegates who presented country reports made it necessary to trim the length of time allowed for these breakout sessions, the participants made significant progress in establishing consensus on issues and forming global networks of contacts in the project management field.

Participants were asked to choose among the following topics:
- Session 1: Global PMBOK
- Session 2: International Project Management Standards
- Session 3: Global Project Management Certification
- Session 4: Global Communications among Project management Professionals and Organizations
- Session 5: Global Project Management Cooperation and Organizational Issues.

In each group, the participants followed the same basic plan for discussion of their topics. they attempted to:
- Identify main issues
- Identify a set of concrete objectives
- Identify major constraints
- Identify a set of steps for achieving the objectives
- Identify a "working group" to continue the discussion/plans after the 1995 Global Forum
- Set a schedule for followup actions and meetings
- Summarize their results on a transparency for presentation to the entire assembly.

The results of these sessions were presented by each group's facilitators during the Plenary session at the end of the forum. Brief descriptions of the work of each group are included on the pages that follow. For more information, or to join a "working group," please contact one of the facilitators.

GLOBAL PROJECT MANAGEMENT BODY OF KNOWLEDGE

Facilitated by Dan Ono, PMI, and Alan Stretton, AIPM

SOME TWENTY PEOPLE participated in this breakout session. Discussion was wide-ranging, but no clearly defined patterns emerged. The broader results could be summarized as follows:
- An effort should be made to develop a core body of knowledge which would find general acceptance globally
- All the country representatives at the Global Forum would be contacted to ascertain or confirm their interest in participating in such an effort
- Subsequent interactions would be by electronic mail, to be set up and coordinated by Dan Ono.

A smaller number of people who attended a follow-up session later in the day were given copies of a draft document "Towards a Core Framework for Project Management Knowledge," developed by a previous joint PMI/IPMA/AIPM working group chaired by Alan Stretton, and invited to comment on it, initially to Dan Ono.

Contact Information

Dan Ono
415/834-2960 (fax)

Alan Stretton
61-2-498-2242 (fax)

INTERNATIONAL PROJECT MANAGEMENT STANDARDS

Facilitated by Klaus Pannenbäcker, IPMA, and Paul Dinsmore, PMI

THE 12 PARTICIPANTS agreed on the necessity of project management standards for education and training, certifications, and accreditation.

Standards describe the today's knowledge and experience of project management as a minimum level of common understanding and acknowledgment.

The working group answered the following questions in keywords.

- What is/are project management standard(s)?
  - Criteria
  - Attributes
  - Principles
  - Practices
  - Guidelines.
- For what/whose purposes project management standards are required?
  - Uniform
  - Consistency
  - Measure
  - Communication
  - Performance
  - Identification
  - Acceptance.
- How to define/revise project management standards globally?
  - Stratify
  - Collect + evaluate + compare under ISO 10006/7 in independent and governing body.

The Project Management Body of Knowledge (PMBOK) is considered as the first project management standard and should be further developed to a Global PMBOK as the basis for future project management standards.

Contact Information

Klaus Pannenbäcker
49-42-13-39-8993 (phone/fax)

Paul Dinsmore: 55-21-252-1200 (fax)
dinsmore@amcham.com.br

GLOBAL PROJECT MANAGEMENT CERTIFICATIONS

Details of this breakout session were unavailable at press time. For information about the session, contact one of these participants:

Contact Information

Kent Crawford
513/748-4060 (fax)
jkcpmsin@infinet.com

Pierre Menard
514/987-3084 (fax)

Jim Klanke
816/524-4625 (fax)

COMMUNICATIONS AMONG PROJECT MANAGEMENT PROFESSIONALS AND ORGANIZATIONS

Facilitated by Thor Gudmundsson, IPMA, Lesley Lindberg, PMI, and Brian Fletcher, PMI

THESE NOTES/MINUTES were completed and refined on the second day. They are also intended to more clearly define an action plan and to be used for requesting feedback comment from the full ad hoc Communications team, likely to be expanded.

Present were: Derek Blue, Cathy Tonne, Jim Lyon, Rehan Ul Ambia Riaz , Norina Finley, Bassam T. Al-Tamimi, Terry Deacon, Lorraine Rieger, Laraine Lippe, Jose Neves, Vijay Verma, Richard Kimball, Thor Gudmundsson, Lesley Lindberg and Brian Fletcher.

A flip chart was used to capture comments and provided the basis for these notes.

Introduction

The working group adopted the following framework for action.
- Identify the main issues.
- Identify a concrete set of objectives.
- Identify the major constraints.
- Identify a set of steps to meet the objectives.
- Identify a working group to continue beyond the '95 Forum.
- Set a schedule for follow-up actions and conferences.

Brian Fletcher and Dick Kimball conducted the brainstorming session, Lesley Lindberg agreed to record the conclusion points and Brian Fletcher agreed to lead the working group of Gudmundsson, Kimball, Lindberg and Fletcher.

Time was limited and in the minutes available, all intended agenda items were not fully addressed. However, it is intended that work should continue throughout the following months. A mechanism will be found to continue exchanges based on the work done already and achieve group consensus.

Findings at the meeting can be summarized as:

Objectives
- To increase awareness and understanding of cultural and environmental issues
- To provide a mechanism for improved communication between project management professionals and organizations.

These objectives are to be accomplished before the Paris Congress in June 1996. Two suggested aspects to consider in this time period are:
- To build the communication structure.
- To provide improved networking opportunities and increase networking.

The Main Issues

The following were proposed as issues to be addressed during discussion.
- Cultural issues:
  - Styles of communication.
  - Perceptions/trust.
  - Building up relationships.
  - Educate/increase understanding.
  - Acceptance, honoring and respect.
  - Strive for neutrality.
- Language issues:
  - Identify and understand language barriers, improve wherever possible, minimize their effects
  - Lessen impact of language barriers through a standard glossary and better interpretation methods
  - Identify, understand and utilize Internet facilities.
- Environmental issues:
  - Timing and time factors.
  - Geographic
  - Political.
- Constraints:
  - Time resource limitation (volunteers)
  - Economical issues
  - Motivation
  - Sensitivity in understanding, sender- receiver.
  - Distance.
  - Emerging technology.

Implementation Plan/Steps

The group recommended that all five Global Forum Working Groups use a web site. All Global Forum Working Groups should be contacted to set up working page to be transmitted to the systems administrator.

Contact Information

Brian Fletcher
905/637-3129 (fax)
76472.1101@compuserve.com

Thor Gudmundsson
47-67-53-13-40 (fax)
controlb@oslonett.no

Lesley Lindberg
204/883-2784 (phone)

GLOBAL PROJECT MANAGEMENT COOPERATION AND ORGANIZATION

Facilitated by Bruce Rodrigues, PMI-South Africa, and Brian Kooyman, AIPM

Main Issues
- Concrete objectives
- Steps to achieve
- Follow up actions/meetings.
- Major constraints
- Working group

Other Issues
- Cultural
- Domestic/global balance
- Open communication channels (Priority B)
- Transition process (Priority A)
- Rights to intellectual properties
- Complexity of design/implementation
- Sincerity between organizations
- Conflicts—standards/certifications, etc.
- Conflicting objectives—synergy/expectations (Priority C)
- Commitment and time.
- National
- Hidden agendas
- Copyright
- Other stakeholders
- Turf/area of geographical activity
- Funding
- ISO relationships
- Language

Transition Process
Objectives:
- To move from diversified groups to global unified organizations with common standards.

Constraints:
- Funding
- Obtaining consensus
- Communications.
- Resistance to change
- Representation and control

Steps:
- Understand current position
- Develop shared vision (benchmarking)
- Obtain stakeholder buy-in
- Execution plan
- Approvals and funding
- Implementation.

Open Communication

Objectives:
- Identify participants
- Establish agreed roles and steps for communication
- Identify practical forms (e-mail, fax, phones)
- Maintain formal regular communication.

Constraints:
- Language translation
- Culture
- Technology available.

Steps:
- Use national delegates as initial point of contact
- Identify information/coordinator.

Contact Information

Lowell S. Skelton, PMI
414/931-4356 (fax)

George T. Patton, PMI
703/920-3127 (fax)

Philip Morin, PMI-Canada
613/824-2783 (phone)
psmorin@magi.com

Michel Brix, PMI-France
33-14-903-2376 (fax)

Joan Chapin, PMI
503/527-5963 (fax)

Richard E. Walz, PMI
214/604-9976 (fax)

Jean Amiot, PMI, PMI-Canada
514/334-6043 (fax)
Jean_A@MKSINFO.QB.CA

Jim Lyon, WAPMA
61-9-385-3849 (fax)

Stephen Harrison, PMI-NZ
64-9-278-6023 (fax)

Serge Rochette, PMI-Canada
416/345-2986

Roger Glaser, PMI
rbglaser@dol.com

Team Members

Brian Kooyman, AIPM
61-2-959-4338 (fax)

Hiroshi Tanaka, ENAA (Japan)
81-45-721-7333 (fax)
tanaka.01818@oct.jgc.co.jp

Bob Kimmons, PMI
713/626-8533 (phone/fax)

Bruce Rodrigues, PMI-SA
27-11-463-1022 (phone/fax)
brucerp@pixie.co.za

Bill Ruggles, PMI-USA
201/749-6064 (fax)
76512.1725@compuserve.com

Marcio Prieto, PMI
55-11-821-5648 (fax)

John Rickards, PMI-Canada
403/281-0725 (fax)
rickards@canuck.com

Dave Florence, PMI
604/487-0356 (phone/fax)
fpm@col.powell.river.bc.ca

PART IV

CONCLUSIONS AND NEXT STEPS

CONTACTS

Note: Telephone numbers NOT preceded by a + are located in the U.S. or Canada.

ARGENTINA
Orlando Marone, PMI
+54-1-379-0318 (tel.)

AUSTRALIA
Brian Kooyman, AIPM
+61-2-959-4338 (fax)

Jim Lyon, WAPMA
+61-9-385-3849 (fax)

Bruce Harper, PMI
+61-3-321-3204 (tel.)

BAHAMAS
Leonard S. Adderley, PMI
809-326-8398 (tel.)

BRAZIL
Marcio Prieto, PMI
+55-11-821-5522 (fax)

Jose Augusto Neves
+55-21-252-1200 (fax)

Paul Dinsmore, PMI Fellow
+55-21-252-1200 (fax)
dinsmore@amcham.com.br

BELGIUM
Jean Compere
+32-2-728-2668 (fax)

Jim Roofthooft, PMI
+32-2-727-9492

CANADA
David Smith, PMI-Canada
403-281-3068 (fax)

Eric Ferland, PMI
418-833-6490 (tel.)

Gabriel Chiniara, PMI
514-345-1655 (tel.)

Lesley Lindberg, PMI
204-883-2784 (tel.)

Ken Parker, PMI
403-493-6850 (tel.)

Gary Graham, PMI
613-957-9766 (tel.)

S.L. Stevenson, PMI
613-584-3311 (tel.)

Waleed Jazrawi, PMI
403-281-5833 (tel.)

Romeo Mitchell, PMI
416-752-1930 (tel.)

Pieter Vannierop, PMI
604-526-3455 (tel.)

Paul V. Gervais, PMI
514-289-8847 (tel.)

Velvet Warrior, PMI
604-389-3515

Alistair MacKenzie, PMI
416-979-5000 (tel.)

John Rickards, PMI
306-665-5103 (tel.)

Michael O'Sullivan, PMI
705-682-5972 (tel.)

CHILE
Pedro Guerra
+55-21-252-1200 (fax)

COLOMBIA
Carlos Gorricho
+57-2-558-4333 (tel.)

CZECH REPUBLIC
Roman Chudoba, PMMS
+42-421-339-8993 (fax)

EGYPT
Ahmed Seif El Din, MES
+20-2-340-1345 (fax)

FRANCE
Michel Brix, PMI-France
+33-1-4903-2836 (tel.)

GERMANY
Klaus Pannenbäcker, IPMA
Olaf Pannenbäcker, GPM
+49-421-339-8993 (fax)

Jens Grappendorf, PMI
+49-69-630-9256 (tel.)

INDIA
Adesh Jain, PMA
+91-11-646-4481 (fax)

Raj Jain, PMI
+91-33-406-254 (tel.)

INDONESIA
Nugget F. Gunawi, PMI
+62-021-725-1966 (tel.)

John Tjahjadi, PT Dacrea
+62-21-5738329 (fax)

ITALY
David Mathie, ANIMP
+39-11-986-3200 (fax)

Moreno Muffato, PMI
+39-49-827-6725 (tel.)

Nicola Colella, PMI
+39-80-548-2471 (tel.)

IRELAND
Ed Naughton, IPM
+353-1-661-3588 (fax)

ISRAEL
Tzvi Raz, PMI-Israel
+972-3-640-9560 (fax)

JAPAN
Hiroshi Tanaka, ENAA
+81-45-721-7333

KOREA
Jong Shin Kim, PROMAT
+82-2-510-5380 (fax)

KUWAIT
Hashem Al-Tabtabi, Kuwait University
+965-481-7424 (fax)

MALAYSIA
Marhalim B. Mustafa, PMI
+60-3-263-2333 (tel.)

Ramasamy Masilamani
+60-3-825-8755 (fax)

The Global Status of the  Project Management Profession

MEXICO
Oscar de Lasse, Calpan SA
+52-5-662-4705 (fax)

Lillian Poulet, PMI
+52-66-84-8401 (tel.)

Benito Morales
+52-5-606-00-1 (tel.)

Luis E. Cancino
+52-961-502.00 (tel.)

Rodrigo Higuera
+52-961- 544.82 (fax)

NEW ZEALAND
Stephen Harrison, PMI-NZ
+64-9-278-6023 (fax)

NIGERIA
Julius Soares, PMI
+234-1-614-092 (tel.)

NORWAY
Thor Gudmundsson, NPMA, IPMA
+47-67-53-13-40 (fax)

PAKISTAN
Rehan ul Ambia Riaz
+92-21-568-2645 (fax)

PERU
J. Felix Valdez, PMI
+51-1-470-6000 (tel.)

RUSSIA
Vladimir Voropajev, SOVNET, IPMA
+7-095-133-2441 (fax)

SAUDI ARABIA
Khalid Alagil, PMI-Arabian Gulf
+966-3-875-4664 (fax)

SINGAPORE
Ed Godycki, PMI
+65-323-7509 (tel.)

SOUTH AFRICA
Pieter Oosthuizen, PMI-South Africa
+27-11-626-1089 (fax)

SPAIN
Alfonso Bucero Torres, Hewlett-Packard Espanola, SA
+43-1-631-18-30 (fax)

SWEDEN
Anders Osterlin, ABB
+46-21-325776

TAIWAN
Robert Lo, PMI
510-254-6908 (tel.)

TURKEY
Ahmet Taspinar, PMI-Northern California
+1-510-569-4636 (fax)

Murat Denzig, PMI
+90-312-385-1900 (tel.)

Mehmet Yehinmen, PMI
+90-212-175-0321 (tel.)

UKRAINE
Victor S. Moskalenko, PMI
215-580-3573 (tel.)

UNITED KINGDOM
Peter W.G. Morris, APM
+44-171-259-0167 (fax)

Louis Prastitis, PMI
+44-171-725-8906 (tel.)

UNITED STATES
David Pells, PMI
+1-214-788-1733(fax)

Roger Glaser, PMI
+1-619-747-2150 (fax)

PMI Executive Office
+1-610-734-3266(fax)
pmieo@ix.netcom.com

VENEZUELA
Lorenzo Caldentey, PMI
+58-1-471-2277(fax)

Jose-Victor Pellisa, PMI
+58-2-442-3897 (tel.)

GLOBAL FORUM SURVEY RESULTS

Submitted by Emma Mathie with the help of David Mathie, Brian Fletcher, and Ahmed Seif El Din

During the morning session of the Global Forum, a small informal survey was conducted to gain an insight into the participants' interpretation of the event and their expectations from it.

The results of the survey were arrived at during the course of the Global Forum breakout sessions. Because of the time constraints, the people constraints (as most of the work was done by two people, David Mathie and Emma Mathie), and the nature of the information gathered, these results are as accurate as circumstances permitted.

The information that follows is meant to give an indication of the various expectations that were identified. Keeping in mind that ideas often change, it is interesting to document what the expectations of the participants were at the beginning of the day.

The starting point was a discussion among friends about what they thought would come out of the Global Forum. As a result, a few questions were asked and further defined to the point where they could be to proposed to the rest of the participants. David Pells, during a break in the morning program, asked participants to record and pass in their answers to these questions:

1. What results would you like to see from today's Global Forum:
    a) today?
    b) one year from now?

2. Are you willing to help make it happen?

The survey was received with enthusiasm and the response rate was very high:
- 110 responses out of 167 attendees, in other words 66 percent.

As can be seen, the questions were straightforward, especially question number two where a simple yes/no answer was expected. However, question number one implied a more complex response and, in fact, answers varied considerably. The themes identified are partly the result of our interpretation of these answers, however, as far as we could determine, these fitted into six broad categories, or themes, which are shown in Table 1 on the following page.

The Global Status of the Project Management Profession

TABLE 1. Six Differing Groups of Opinions Motivated the Participants' Expectations of the Day's Global Forum

1. NETWORKING	29
2. GLOBAL FORUM	27
3. CULTURAL IMPLICATIONS	26
4. FORMAL FEDERATION	11
5. PRODUCTS	11
6. ENHANCEMENT OF THE PROFESSION	6
TOTAL	**110**

An analysis of the findings shows that these six differing groups of opinions motivated the participants' expectations of the day's Global Forum. Through most of them held the same ideal of Internationalization, networking seemed to be the most important thought the morning session. If a Global Forum were established as an annual event, networking would be a by-product, as would be the opportunity to experience cultural exchanges.

The desire to establish an annual Global Forum that would enhance the globalization of project management was the second most popular interest. It should be noted that Internationalization could also occur by means of a Formal Federation (ranked #4 among the interest areas).

The aim of yet another sub-group was to use the Forum to help with the globalization of PM standards, exemplified by the PMBOK product. Enhancement of the profession, interest area #6 could be better achieved if the profession is international than if it remains an effort segmented into national organizations that do not share information, ideals and goals.

Table 2 shows the ranked answers to question 1b).

TABLE 2. Answers to Question Two in Ranked Order.

1. GLOBAL FORUM	46
2. PRODUCTS	30
3. FORMAL FEDERATION	22
4. NETWORKING	12
TOTAL	**110**

Comparing the immediate expectations with longer-term ones, a few trends begin to manifest themselves. Maintaining the Global Forum as a constant feature of the PMI symposia, and/or is the main expectation of the survey group. This is the logical first step, because it aids the creation of international products and the aim of international networking. As regards the distinction between Global Forum and Formal Federation, it remains to be established whether this is distinction of form or content, but at this stage it is impossible to define.

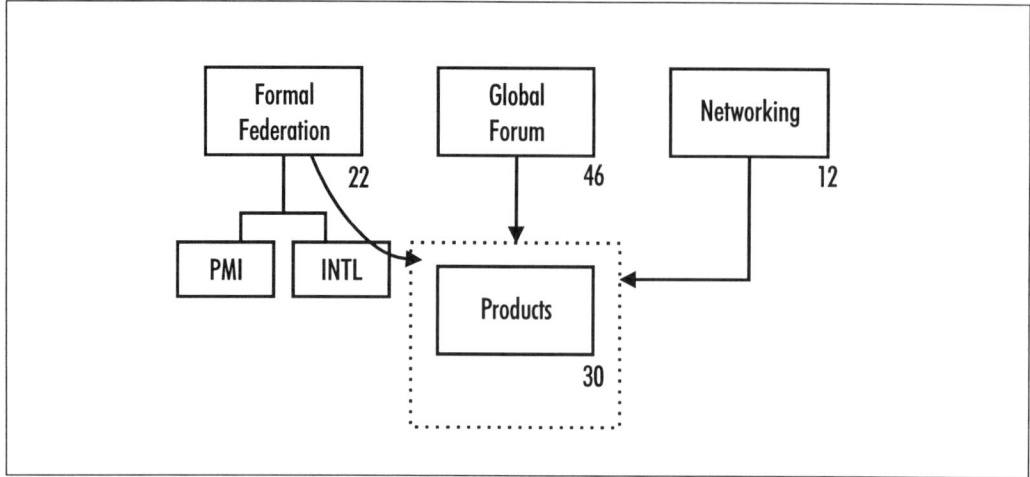

The overall results from this informal survey can be graphically represented like the illustration above.

This diagram expresses what was difficult to represent with the earlier strict categorizations. As answers were not always so definite, but overlapped and complemented one another, this represents a necessary addition to the above analysis.

From the diagram it is possible to see that, whether looking for Internationalization by means of a Global Forum or a Formal Federation, or simply looking for more opportunities to network, the interest of the participants is in any case focused on the achievement of international products and contacts.

Answers to Question Two

In response to the second part of the questionnaire the majority of the people present answered that YES they would be willing to help make it happen. Indeed the commitment shown during the breakout sessions, and in following up on them is an auspicious way to start.

HOW TO PARTICIPATE

INDIVIDUALS AND ORGANIZATIONS are invited to participate in the globalization of the project management profession in the following ways:

Project Management Associations
To join a project management professional association in your country or region, contact the appropriate representative identified on pages 165–166 of this report. If none is listed for your area, feel free to contact IPMA in Europe or PMI in North America.

National Project Management Activities and Events

Global Working Groups

Future Country Reports

Future Global Project Management Forums
See pages 168–169.

Global Project Management Forums on the World Wide Web (Internet)

Corporate Sponsorship

For more information, contact:
David Pells
Tel:(+1-214)788-1873
Fax:(+1-214)788-1733

The Global Status of the Project Management Profession

IPMA '96 GLOBAL PM FORUM

Paris, France • Sunday, 23 June 1996

EVENT: Second Global Project Management Forum
First follow-up to the First Global PM Forum in New Orleans. One-day event preceding IPMA '96 World Congress on Project Management

DESCRIPTION: Representatives of all known project management associations around the world invited to participate, present status of the PM profession, and discuss issues of common interest.

AGENDA: Speeches, breakout discussion sessions, reception

DATE: Sunday, 23 June, 1996

LOCATION: CNIT Conference Center, Paris-La Défense
Five minutes from Champs-Elysées, Paris, France

SPONSORS: International Project Management Association (IPMA)
Association Française du Management de Projet

CONTACTS: Klaus Pannenbäcker, IPMA
Tel: (+49-421)339-8993
Fax: (+49-421)339-8993

COST: To Be Determined

The Global Status of the Project Management Profession

PMI '96
GLOBAL PM FORUM

Boston, Massachusetts, USA • 9-10 October 1996

EVENT:	Third Global Project Management Forum First PMI-sponsored follow-up to the Global PM Forum held in New Orleans at PMI '95. Two-day event immediately following PMI '96 Seminar/Symposium in Boston
SUMMARY:	Representatives of all known project management associations around the world are invited to participate, present status of the project management profession, and discuss issues of common interest. • Panel discussions by industry leaders • Presentations on global, multinational initiatives • Globally recognized speakers invited to address Global Forum • Group discussions on global project management issues
AGENDA:	Wednesday: Speeches, Status Reports, Int'l Reception Thursday: Panel Discussions, Presentations, Breakouts
DATE:	Wednesday, 9 October 1996 • 1–5:30 p.m. Thursday, 10 October 1996 • 8–5:00 p.m.
LOCATION:	Boston Convention Center Boston, Massachusetts, USA
SPONSORS:	Project Management Institute (PMI) International Project Management Association (IPMA)
CONTACTS:	Brian Fletcher Tel:(+1-905)637-5864 Fax:(+1-905)637-3129 76472.1101compuserve.com David Pells Tel:(+1-214)788-1873 Fax:(+1-214)788-1733
COST:	To Be Determined

All PM professionals and members of the pubic are welcome.

The Global Status of the Project Management Profession

PART V
SPONSORS OF THE 1995 GLOBAL FORUM

The Global Status of the Project Management Profession

BellSouth

Carter & Burgess, Inc.

The Global Status of the 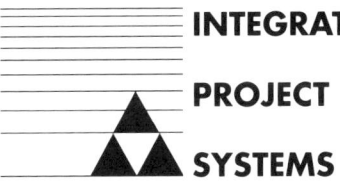 Project Management Profession

INTEGRATED PROJECT SYSTEMS
Project Management Solutions for High Technology Environments

High technology companies win if they create winning products. But delivering the right product, at the right time, at the right cost is increasingly difficult as product life-cycles grow shorter, competition looms larger, and development teams are spread farther around the globe!

The more complex your development efforts become, the more you need an integrated approach to project management. Integrated Project Systems has a solution that integrates people, processes, and tools so they all work together. This approach has been tested and proven to result in more predictable and credible schedules, less rework, and more productive people for some of today's most successful technology companies! If you'd like to hear more about how your company can deliver better products, in less time, at lower costs — call Integrated Project Systems at 415-802-1020.

The Global Status of the Project Management Profession

NCR

"Bringing Order to Project Chaos"

Why NCR for Project Management

- NCR has global capability and worldwide resources who have managed large, complex projects

- NCR has industry experience and expertise

- NCR maintains a leadership position in the project management profession

Why GlobalPM™ Methodology

- GlobalPM is a proven, flexible methodology employing "best practices" techniques

- GlobalPM is a worldwide methodology with an emphasis on results

- GlobalPM establishes the project manager as a single point of contact

Copyright © 1996
By NCR
Dayton, OH USA
All Rights Reserved

The Global Status of the Project Management Profession

START YOUR PROJECT RIGHT!
WITH ENOUGH MONEY!

PROJECT DEVELOPMENT & FINANCING SERVICES FOR CRITICAL PROJECTS IN DEVELOPING ECONOMIES

SERVICES

1. Business Development Services
   (Representing US businesses seeking new projects internationally)
2. Project Packaging Services
   (Planning, Structuring, Documenting & Packaging Major Projects for Financing Purposes Including all necessary Feasibility Studies, Financial Analysis & Organizational Documents)
3. Project Financing Services
   (Presentations to investors in the USA and Europe, including debt, equity, and lease financing, based on relationships with government funds, equity funds, and banks)
4. Project Management Services
   (Assistance during project implementation, including financial management, oversight, contract management, planning, reporting and organizational facilitation)
5. Project Investments
   (We invest in selected projects for our own account, and for client investors)

GEOGRAPHIC EXPERIENCE

Eastern Europe:	Hungary, Slovakia, Czech Republic, Estonia, Latvia, Lithuania
Russia & NIS:	Russia, Ukraine
Latin America:	Mexico, Colombia, Brazil

TYPES OF PROJECTS

Property Development:	Industrial Facilities, Hotels, Offices, Mixed Usage, Warehousing
Infrastructure:	Russia, Ukraine
Oil & Gas:	Exploration, Pipelines, Processing, Transportation

WE ORGANIZE THE TEAM, PACKAGE THE PROJECT, ARRANGE FINANCING & DELIVER THE PROJECT.
— REDUCING RISKS ALL AROUND —
— INSURING SUCCESS —

For more information on company services and fees, or for a question for a specific project, contact company offices at the following:

Strategic Project Development, Inc.
12001 N. Central Expressway, Suite 340
Dallas, Texas, 75243, USA
Tel: (1-214)788-1830   Fax: (1-214)788-1733

University of San Diego
School of Business Administration
Graduate Programs

- MASTER OF BUSINESS ADMINISTRATION
- MASTER OF INTERNATIONAL BUSINESS
- EMPHASIS IN PROGRAM/PROJECT MANAGEMENT AVAILABLE
- CERTIFICATE PROGRAM IN PROJECT MANAGEMENT

Accredited by the American Assembly of Collegiate Schools of Business (AACSB)

Evening Classes
Full and Part-time Study
Enter Fall, Spring, Summer

University of San Diego

OFFICE OF GRADUATE ADMISSIONS
5998 Alcalá Park, San Diego, CA 92110-2492
(619) 260-4524   Fax (619) 260-4891

PART VI

ATTENDEES OF THE 1995 GLOBAL FORUM

The Global Status of the Project Management Profession

ATTENDEES

Wayne Abba, USA
John Adams, USA
Wayne Alphonso, USA
Hashem Al-Tabtabi, Kuwait
Bassan Al-Tamimi, Saudi Arabia
Khalid Alagil, Saudi Arabia
Jean Amiot, Canada
Mark Aukeman, USA
Richard Balfour, Canada
Kumar Bhagavatheswaran, USA
Deborah Bigelow, USA
Thomas Block, USA
Derek Blue, Canada
Michel Brix, France
Jeannette Cabanis, USA
Lorenzo Caldentey, Venezuela
Lisa Camstra, USA
Page Carter, USA
Joan Chapin, USA
Roman Chudoba, Czech Republic
David Cleland, USA
Curtis Cook, USA
Helen Cooke, USA
Kent Crawford, USA
Terence Deacon, South Africa
Oscar De Lasse, Mexico
Mary Devon-O'Brien, USA
Lars Sam Dholm, Denmark
Don Dible, USA
Paul Dinsmore, Brazil
Sharon Feeley, USA
Norina Finley, USA
Brian Fletcher, Canada
Kevin Fletcher, Canada
David Florence, Canada
Masatake Futami, Japan
Cherrie Geerdts, USA
Roger Glaser, USA
Earl Glenwright, USA
Myla Goldman, USA

Carlos Gorricho, Colombia
John Grant, USA
Thorhallur Gudmundsson, Norway
Joseph Guella, USA
Pedro Guerra, Chile
Leland Guth, USA
Michael Haig, USA
Grace Hamion
Stephen Harrison, New Zealand
Kenneth Hartley, USA
Judith Hayes, USA
Celine Goodine Hellberg
Carl Isenberg, USA
Elvin Isgrig, USA
Adesh Jain, India
Robert Janowski
Eric Jenett, USA
Inhwah Joh, Korea
John Kennel, USA
William Kern, USA
Shunji Kido, Japan
Jong Shin Kim, Korea
Sooyeun Kim, Korea
Richard Kimball, USA
Robert Kimmons, USA
James Klanke, USA
Yoshiaki Konishi, Japan
Brian Kooyman, Australia
Ian Leslie, Australia
Ralph Levene, England
Lesley Lindberg, Canada
Robert W. Lindemann, USA
Laraine Lippe, USA
Dana Littlefield, USA
Lyle Lockwood, USA
Roger Lowe, Canada
James Lyon, Australia
Raymond Mak, USA
Rodrigo Manautou, Mexico
Mike Manion, USA
Lary Mars, USA
Michael Martin, USA
Emma Mathie, Italy
David Mathie, Italy

Bryan McConachy, Canada
John McGill, USA
Pierre Menard, Canada
Ramasamy Masilamani, Malaysia
Akio Mitsufuji, Japan
Philip Morin, Canada
Peter Morris, England
Masao Motegi, Japan
Koji Nakamoto, Japan
Ed Naughton, Ireland
Jose Neves, Chile
George Newby, USA
Michael Newell, USA
Saralee Newell, USA
Tsuneo Noguchi, Japan
Dan Ono, USA
Pieter Oosthuizen, South Africa
Anders Osterlin, Sweden
Gerald Ostrander, USA
Klaus Pannenbäcker, Germany
Olaf Pannenbäcker, Germany
Ken Parker, Canada
George T. Patton, USA
David Pells, USA
James Pennypacker, USA
Christine Petitgras, France
Louis Prastitis, England
Marcio Prieto, Brazil
Louis Prudhomme, USA
Merritt Ranstead, USA
Rehan ul ambia Riaz, Pakistan
John Rickards, Canada
Constance Riedinger, USA
Lorraine Rieger, USA
Serge Rochette, Canada
Bruce Rodrigues, South Africa
William Ruggles, USA
Gerald Salcher, Canada
Karl Arne Samuelssen, Sweden
Mark Scheinberg, USA

Jette Schramm-Nielsen, Denmark
David Scott, USA
Ahmed Seif El Din, Egypt
Gunnar Selin, Sweden
Lowell S. Skelton, USA
James Smith, USA
John Smith, USA
William Snow, USA
Alan Stretton, Australia
Michio Takahashi, Japan
Kazumi Takei, Japan
Billy Wai Keung Tam, Hong Kong
Katsumi Tamura, Japan
Hiroshi Tanaka, Japan
Ahmet Taspinar, USA and Turkey
Charles Teplitz, USA
Yosuke Terawaki, Japan
Geoffrey Thomas, USA
Robert Thompson, USA
John Tjahjadi, Indonesia
Alfonso Bucero Torres, Spain
Catherine Tonne, USA
William Trnka, USA
Brian Urwin, Australia
Tom Vanderheiden, USA
Vijay Verma, Canada
Mary Vincent, USA
Maria Voropaeva, Russia
Vladimir Voropajev, Russia
Ronald Waller, USA
Richard Walz, USA
Walter Wawruck, Canada
Stephen Wearne, England
Francis Webster, USA
Barbara Wheeler, USA
Karen White, USA
Rush Williamson, Jr., USA
Barbara Wong, USA
Tony Woodrich, USA
Naoki Yamada, Japan
Robert Youker, USA
Alaa Zeitoun, USA
Rene Zuazo, USA